Chronology of Education
in the United States

Chronology of Education in the United States

RUSSELL O. WRIGHT

McFarland & Company, Inc., Publishers
Jefferson, North Carolina, and London

LIBRARY OF CONGRESS CATALOGUING-IN-PUBLICATION DATA

Wright, Russell O.
    Chronology of education in the United States / Russell O.
Wright.
        p.   cm.
    Includes bibliographical references and index.

    ISBN 0-7864-2502-4 (softcover : 50# alkaline paper) ∞

    1. Education — United States — History — Chronology.
I. Title.
LA205.W75   2006
370.9'0202 — dc22   2006003244

British Library cataloguing data are available

Cover photograph ©2006 Veer.com

Manufactured in the United States of America

*McFarland & Company, Inc., Publishers
    Box 611, Jefferson, North Carolina 28640
    www.mcfarlandpub.com*

To Doris Mae Wright Beck

CONTENTS

ACKNOWLEDGMENTS

What I have previously called the Wright writing company again played a major role in the writing of this book, the seventh in a series of chronologies.

My wife, Halina Wright, provided research assistance through the Internet, our local library, and the *Los Angeles Times*. She also acted as a first-class editor when reviewing the manuscript.

My daughter, Terry Ann Wright, worked her Microsoft Word magic to create the manuscript, including the figures in the appendix and the arrangement of the index. She was also the primary Internet researcher, demonstrating a master of the Web gained through years of experience. With just a wisp of information, she can supply many pages of detailed reportage on seemingly any subject or name. In the hands of a careful researcher with Terry's expertise, the Internet is an invaluable tool for tracking down almost any information that one desires. Terry also made any recommendations on the content of this book based upon her experiences in classrooms and as an assistant to college professors during pursuit of her master's degree.

I must again note the contributions of my sons, Dan and Brian Wright, who provided the expertise needed to keep our personal computers and peripherals operating and up to date. Also, they and their sons, Brian and Christopher respectively, provided much-needed help in surviving a change of residence that came right at the most crucial time in the final completion of the book.

INTRODUCTION

The word "education" is derived from a Latin word meaning leading, or drawing out. In a natural sense, any organism is educated by environmental pressures to take actions that give it a higher probability of survival. In the sense that we most often use the word today, education is an organized attempt to impart knowledge, skills, and ways of thinking that are considered valuable to the existing society, and thus desirable for maturing members of the society to learn. This means that education takes different forms depending on what a specific society considers important to be learned, and which gender should learn what (in many societies it is not thought necessary or even desirable to provide the same education to females as is provided to males — or to provide any organized education to females at all).

For many centuries, education was available only to the relatively elite classes of society, and then only to the males of that class. Often the "education" consisted primarily of being directed how to follow orders from on high. Charlemagne, who ruled around 800 ad, has to be credited with making the most significant effort to provide educational opportunities for children of all classes of society in Europe.

But the concept of education for all was an idea that grew very slowly in the world. Authoritarian regimes (including religious ones) were suspicious of "too much" education that could cause subjects to question blind obedience to authority. By the time settlers arrived in America in the early 1600s, they had resolved these issues among themselves, primarily in favor of nearly universal education. However, there were still questions about the degree of education that should be made available to females, especially above elementary educational levels.

This chronology covers the development of education in Colonial America and the United States since 1600, when those new settlers began arriving. Education in the United States, at least in concept, has evolved

1

today to the point where it is considered desirable to provide all children present in the country, citizen or not, handicapped or not, with a free basic education regardless of gender, race, or ethnic background. Similarly, higher education is available without restrictions to all adults who can afford it and can meet the academic requirements of the institution providing the higher education.

As in any human endeavor, there are gaps between the basic concept and the manner in which that concept is executed in practice, but education is currently believed to be of great importance in the United States. It is mandatory for all children until a certain age. In an era of globalization, the majority of Americans believe that the success of any nation is proportional to the degree to which its inhabitants are educated and thus capable of performing the tasks necessary to sustain the economy. This chronology records how, amid many conflicts of opinion along the way, we have arrived at this conclusion about the purposes of education.

The Magnitude of the Educational Process in the United States

There are about 55 million children enrolled in public and private elementary and secondary schools (up to grade 12) in the United States. If we add teachers and staff and the about 16 million adults involved in higher education, we get a total of about 78 million people. This means that over one in every four persons in the United States is either learning in school, teaching, or working in school administration in some capacity. This does not include the parents who are following the progress of the education of their children, nor any of the people providing teaching materials, etc., to the schools. Education in the United States is truly a massive undertaking.

If we took just the 78 million people actually learning in school or working there as the total population of a country, that country would be the fifteenth most populous country in the world. With an educational system of this magnitude, it is not surprising that the process is often the subject of passionate debate concerning goals, results, and perceived necessary improvements. Further, with laws carefully crafted to make education freely accessible to literally everyone in certain age groups, it is not surprising than many lawsuits are brought by those who believe the educational process is failing to meet its intended goals. Throughout the history of education in the United States, legal conflict has accompanied the evolution of the educational process. That conflict is detailed throughout the chronology.

Perhaps the best way to provide an overview of the development of the education process in the United States is to consider separately the development of the public elementary and secondary schools, the development of postsecondary higher education, and finally the interplay of the actions of the federal government and state governments. The individual states have the basic responsibility for education, but the federal government has become deeply involved because it bears the responsibility for deciding constitutional issues. Further, the efforts of the federal government to help provide funding and direction to the educational process generally come with strings attached. This issue will be reviewed after considering the development of education through the secondary and postsecondary levels.

The Development of Elementary and Secondary Education

The elementary and secondary educational systems in the United States today are divided between various "grades." Since the 50 individual states are responsible for basic education in the United States, and most decisions are made at local levels by local school boards, it is remarkable that the educational systems among the states are so similar. But the pressures of preparing students in a standard way for admission to colleges at the postsecondary level, and the need to have an efficient system to process the massive number of pupils to be educated, have both combined to make each state deal with education in a similar way.

The development of elementary and secondary education in the United States was a somewhat haphazard process in colonial times, with different standards applying in different parts of the country. The evolution of this process is described in the next section of this introduction. But a key step that should be noted here was the establishment, around 1860, of the concept of "graded" schools in metropolitan areas. This approach was aimed at replacing "one-room" schools (some of which held up to 200 students in a single room in large cities). The graded-school concept was seen as an efficient way to process a large mass of students. By 1870 the concept had spread nearly everywhere there were enough students to separate into "grades." This approach continued into the twentieth century, with fine-tuning as necessary. Today it seems as if no other system ever existed.

A major fine-tuning step came in 1906 with the creation of the "Carnegie unit." Educators, concerned with the differences between high schools in different places, and attempting to find a standardized way to have those high schools prepare students for college (and to create standardization in the colleges themselves) came up with the Carnegie unit, so-called because it was developed by the Carnegie Foundation for the Advancement of Teaching. The Carnegie unit defined a block of time of about 50–55 daily minutes that was set aside to teach a specific subject five times a week. The subjects were those needed to meet college requirements, and a specific college had to teach a certain number of Carnegie units to qualify to call itself a college. The Carnegie unit was a very convenient measuring stick to compare schools, and it fit very well into the graded system.

Today all states basically operate a K–12 (kindergarten through twelfth grade) system with education compulsory through 12th grade (or the age that corresponds to 12th grade). There are "nursery" schools in many states that offer preschooling to children under five years of age. Most of these are commercial ventures utilized by parents who can afford them, and they are not part of the basic school system. However, under the federal Head Start program, which is specifically targeted to lower-income children, government funds are made available for such schooling, and it is closely coordinated with local school districts.

The official school system starts with kindergarten, which is intended for children who are 5–6 years old. Then, in sequence, first grade covers children aged 6–7, second grade 7–8 years old, third grade 8–9 years old, fourth grade 9–10 years old, fifth grade 10–11 years old, and sixth grade 11–12 years old. Through sixth grade is usually called elementary school. However, in earlier times country schools would go through eight grades, and then a graduation ceremony would be held before the pupils went on to the high school in town to begin ninth grade. Today many schools have a middle school that begins as early as fifth grade and runs through eighth grade. Less commonly now, some systems create a junior high school that covers seventh through ninth grades. Whatever the designation of the schools, seventh grade is for pupils 12–13 years old and eighth grade is for pupils 13–14 years old. Then the typical high school designation starts at ninth grade and is often called freshman year for pupils in the 14–15 age bracket.

Starting the high school designation at ninth grade has grown in popularity because it matches the college sequence of freshman-sophomore-junior-senior. In high school the 10th grade is the sophomore year for pupils 15–16 years old, 11th grade the junior year for 16–17 year olds, and 12th grade the senior year for 17–18-year-old-students. As noted, the grading system was developed around 1860, and it caught on very quickly as an efficient way to process a large number of pupils through the school system.

Some systems proposed grades originally as a way to split six years of elementary school from six years of secondary school in a 6-3-3 system that would include junior and senior high schools in secondary education. Other systems have evolved as noted, but elementary school is still thought of as ending at grade 6, while at the other end high school now usually means grades 9 through 12. Some other systems exist that split the grades even finer, but these are not common.

In their junior year (11th grade), students are expected to take the SAT so that their test results are available when the students apply for college admission during their senior (12th grade) year. The percentage of those who actually graduate from high school that apply to college has varied in the mid–60s for several years, although only 68 percent of those who start ninth grade actually graduate from high school on schedule. The percentage of graduates climbs above 80 percent if one includes students up to 25 years of age who finally complete high school or a General Equivalency Diploma (GED), essentially a test whose satisfactory completion is considered equivalent to graduating from high school.

The percentage of high school graduates applying to college has slowly grown from less than 50 percent before 1960, but this has become an issue in determining the present curriculum to be offered in high school. If only a little less than two-thirds of high school graduates apply to college, then more than one-third of all students do not need a high degree of academic training, according to some critics. But others say that a minimal academic content is necessary for high school graduates to get good jobs in today's complicated globalized economy, whether or not the students plan to apply to college. This argument has actually been going on for more than a century (see further on).

For students who plan to apply for college, Advanced Placement (AP) or International Baccalaureate (IB) courses are available in many high schools. These courses are the equivalent of freshman-year college courses, and many postsecondary schools give unit credits that allow early graduation. College admissions officers give much weight to the results of these courses, thus increasing the chances of admission to colleges with highly competitive admissions policies. Public or private schools in wealthy area tend to have more optional AP or IB courses than public schools in impoverished inner-city schools, thus putting students in such schools at a disadvantage.

Students in the United States can choose between public-funded (free) public schools or private schools for which they must pay (only about 6 percent of students are in private schools). Private schools usually have better facilities and often have smaller class sizes than public schools, especially those public schools located in large cities. Private schools can close admissions at a certain point, but public schools must accept anyone who signs up.

The Evolution of the Present Elementary/Secondary School System

The key history of education in the United States below the college level focuses on secondary education, and more specifically, on the high school.

Elementary education began almost as soon as the early settlers got established, although it took different forms in New England, the mid–Atlantic states, and the South. Children started school at the age of six or seven, and the curriculum consisted of the "four Rs": religion, reading, writing, and arithmetic. New England developed the most formal school system, and such innovations as district schools, compulsory education, and taxation to support schools survive in modified form even today.

As the nation expanded westward, elementary education expanded with it, resulting in a series of one-room schoolhouses spread across the nation, with educational materials such as *McGuffey's Readers* forming the basis of the curriculum. The subject of education did not even appear in the constitution that was adopted in 1789, and the elementary schools developed in a somewhat haphazard fashion until the Civil War ended in 1865. The end of the war added about four million newly freed slaves to the nation's population (then about 35 million, having grown from about 4 million at the end of the Revolutionary War), and the need for educational facilities increased accordingly.

Kindergartens appeared in the 1850s and quickly became very popular, but at the other end of the scale, high schools grew very slowly. The first public high school did not appear until 1821 in Boston, and it was intended only for boys. Gender bias was not a basic issue in elementary schooling because few towns could afford to build separate schoolhouses for girls and boys, and thus both sexes attended school together until they moved into their teens.

By the 1870s, high schools began to enroll girls, many of whom went on to be trained in "normal" schools to become teachers. Many children from working-class families also enrolled in high school to learn a skilled trade. A major event took place when the Michigan Supreme Court ruled in 1874 that taxes could be levied to support public high schools as well as elementary schools. This was an answer to the complaint of those who saw no need for education above the elementary level. As the Industrial Revolution drove the movement of mass urbanization, large cities began to build high schools.

Many of these new high schools featured vocational or "manual" training rather than college preparatory training, although such "college prep" courses were still available. But the prime goal for many students was to be trained to take jobs in the growing factories and agricultural enterprises in the nation (even as late as 1900 only about one-tenth of the students in high school planned to go on to college).

In 1892, a Committee of Ten was appointed by the National Educational Association (NEA) to establish standards for a basic high school curriculum. The NEA had been founded in 1870 by a merger of the National

Teacher's Association with the National Association of School Superinten-
dents and the American Normal School Association. The Committee of Ten
was headed by Harvard president Charles W. Eliot, and consisted of other
college presidents and school leaders.

The committee emphasized the need for mental discipline, and it recommended that all high school students take essentially the same basic academic courses, whether or not they planned to go to college. The committee
felt there should be no distinction between those preparing for college and
those "preparing for life," an expression used by those opposed to high school
curricula that emphasized academic performance.

If this argument sounds familiar, it is because it is still going on today,
even though nearly two-thirds of students who graduate from high school
today do plan to go on to college. The ongoing argument today for "reform"
in this area is one reason the authors of the respected book *History of Education in America*, John D. Pulliam and James L. Van Patten, say in their
seventh edition that "one of the great tragedies of American education is that
we keep inventing the wheel."

A "new wheel" appeared about 25 years after the Committee of Ten
had done their work. New waves of immigrants were coming to the United
States at the time (and continued to do so through the first two decades of
the twentieth century). Many were poor and uneducated and began to fill
the high schools of the United States. Many educators felt the greatest need
in education for these masses, whom the educators felt would go on to
unskilled or semiskilled work after high school, was acculturation to American society.

Further, around 1900 what became known as the progressive movement, whose icon was John Dewey, was claiming that too much learning in
schools was by rote and that "learning by doing" was the proper way for children to learn in school. The Progressive Education Association (PEA) was
founded in 1919, but its influence was felt in schools well before that date.
Similarly, the PEA formally died in 1955, but its influence had waned well
in advance of that date, as by then it was felt to be too "soft" an educational
process.

Another factor was the growth of vocational education in the first two
decades of the twentieth century, with the Smith-Hughes Act of 1917, which
provided federal aid to the states for vocational education, being a major
boost to such education. The act helped pay the salaries of vocational teachers and assisted in their training.

As a result of these and other pressures, the NEA in 1913 appointed a
Commission on the Reorganization of Secondary Education. Five years later,
in 1918, the commission issued *The Cardinal Principles of Secondary Education*, a document that essentially turned the high schools into a vehicle for

social integration and building of values. *The Cardinal Principles* was published by the United States Bureau of Education and became the dominant approach in high schools for the next four decades. The approach became known as "life adjustment" education, although some called it simply "custodial care." The seven cardinal principles were:

1. Health
2. Command of fundamental processes
3. Worthy home membership
4. Vocation
5. Citizenship
6. Worthy use of leisure time
7. Ethical character

High school enrollment rose dramatically in the following decades due to the enactment of child labor laws and truancy laws. In 1890 there were over 200,000 students in 2,500 high schools. By 1900 there were over 500,000 students, and by 1940 there were over six million high school students. Following the tenets of the *Cardinal Principles*, so-called general studies, neither specifically for the college-bound nor for vocational preparation, began to push out the more rigorous academic and/or career/technical disciplines. This situation persisted into the 1940s.

After World War II, in 1945, a report from Harvard College that became known as the "Redbook," and a statement by Charles Prosser, director of the Federal Board for Vocational Education, that became known as the Prosser Resolution, both gave added support to the idea of "life adjustment" education. Educators and the public seemed satisfied with the less rigorous academic approach, even though the number of high school graduates going on to apply for a college education had risen to about 25 percent. This sense of satisfaction was abruptly broken by the shock of *Sputnik* in 1957, but a much bigger shock occurred in 1954, when the Supreme Court ruled that the doctrine of "separate but equal," which had supported segregation up to then, was unconstitutional on its face.

The Shock of Integration

The National Association for the Advancement of Colored People (NAACP) had been working since its formation in 1909 to overturn the Supreme Court decision of 1896 (Plessy) that sanctioned the "separate but equal" doctrine supporting segregation in general, and specifically in the schools of the South. The NAACP had been chipping away at segregation through the first half of the twentieth century by arguing that even if "separate but equal" was a legal approach, schools in the South, particularly higher education law schools, could not remotely claim to offer "equal" educational opportunities to whites and blacks. In fact, some southern states were becoming uneasy because the NAACP was winning a number of small victories with its strategy of forcing southern states either to go to the considerable expense of building truly equal college facilities (which did exist in some places at the elementary/secondary level), or reluctantly to accept some integration at the college level.

The NAACP had been reluctant to try to challenge the "separate but equal" doctrine directly, and many black teachers in segregated schools in some areas were afraid of losing their jobs if the NAACP was successful in forcing integration at the elementary/secondary level. But by 1949 the NAACP had requests from five groups of plaintiffs who wanted to go forward, and the NAACP agreed to help them.

The NAACP tried each case before federal tribunals in their respective districts. All were rejected at the initial level, but some comments were made that the "separate but equal" doctrine should be discarded, but only the Supreme Court could do so. The Supreme Court consolidated the five cases into one, bearing the name of *Brown v. Board of Education*, and thus Brown would become the name by which its historic decision would be known. The combined case was argued and discussed from the end of 1952 through the beginning of 1954. During this time Chief Justice Frederick Vinson died and was replaced by Earl Warren, formerly governor of California. Warren's political skills helped bring a unanimous decision in the case.

The opinion was delivered on May 14, 1954. The decision was that segregation had no valid purpose. It was imposed basically simply to give blacks lower status based on race. Thus, segregation was unconstitutional under the fourteenth Amendment. There were many additional and controversial statements about the psychological damage caused by segregation, but the violation of the equal protection clause of the fourteenth Amendment was the fundamental basis for the ruling.

Realizing the substantial impact of their decision, the justices proposed a delay in implementing the decision until appropriate remedies could be reviewed. This decision was issued in May 1955 (generally called Brown II), and was roundly criticized in retrospect for not issuing specific deadlines for dismantling segregation, but instead using the infamous phrase "with all deliberate speed." The vague phrase became a way for many school districts to deliberately delay the implementation of integration in their districts.

Probably the most famous battle over integration at the elementary/secondary school level came in Little Rock, Arkansas, where President Eisenhower was forced to send in federal troops in the fall of 1957 to enforce integration. The schools were finally closed there for the 1958–59 school year by order of Governor Faubus, an ardent segregationist. But the school board, after a recall election, decided in the spring of 1959 to open the schools again in a few months, well before the closing order issued by Faubus was found in June to be unconstitutional. Integration began again in August 1959, but it took until 1972 for it to be effective at all levels of the elementary/secondary school system.

Integration also was a painful process in many other parts of the nation. Through the next two decades many urban schools experienced de facto segregation as whites fled to the suburbs and blacks filled innercity schools. Some judges tried to use strategies like busing to achieve integration by brute force, but this mostly produced only frustration and anger on both sides, and the Supreme Court primarily struck down attempts to bus students out of cities to the suburbs and viceversa.

One of the most extreme cases of the negative results of the integration battle occurred in Summerton, South Carolina, where the first of the combined Brown cases was filed (commonly known as "Briggs" after the names of two plaintiffs in the case), and where the famous "doll study" by Kenneth Clark was first introduced into evidence. After the 1954 Supreme Court decision, those involved with the Briggs case found it to be a hollow victory.

Rev. Joseph De Laine, acknowledged leader of the black community in Summerton, had his church burned, and he moved to New York in 1955 after an attempted drive-by shooting. Harry and Eliza Briggs, on behalf of whose children the suit was filed, lost their jobs and also moved north. Fifty years after the Supreme Court decision, Summerton's schools remained effectively segregated. Nearly all white students were attending a private school, leaving the public schools almost entirely black.

In spite of cases such as this, integration became the law of the land and has been generally absorbed into the school system, with de facto inner city/suburb segregation remaining as its prime negative effect. Most educational and legal scholars consider the integration decision of 1954 to be the most significant event of the twentieth century in American schools.

The Shocks of Sputnik *and* A Nation at Risk

While the nation was still in turmoil following the integration decisions of 1954 and 1955, the Soviet Union delivered a shock to the high school curriculum debate when it launched *Sputnik* in October 1957. Policymakers of all types and at all levels attacked the high schools as doing an inadequate job of preparing students, especially in math and the sciences, for the task of competing in the Cold War with Russia, and competing in the economic war with newly emerging economic powers Japan and Germany, whom we had defeated in World War II.

More money was poured into schools, but the schools basically continued their "tracking" policies that put different students into different courses based on test scores and the advice of counselors. As one study put it: "The more the schools changed (bigger budgets, better facilities), the more they stayed the same (low academic expectations for the majority)."

The next curriculum shock had a greater impact, even though changes came slowly afterwards. In 1983, the National Commission on Excellence in Education that had been appointed by Secretary of Education Terrence Bell issued a report called *A Nation at Risk*. This report caused a great furor. The commission expressed great alarm that the rise of global trade and the United States as the leading world power, and the beginning of the information age, were not being accompanied by complementary changes in the schools.

A Nation at Risk drew conclusions similar to those of the Committee of Ten in 1892. The philosophy of providing all students with a rigorous academic curriculum was recommended as the new goal for high schools. As a result, nearly all states have raised the number of academic credits required for graduation, and have made academic standards more rigorous. But overall progress has been slow. Even though nearly two-thirds of high school graduates now plan to go on to college, the rate of high school dropouts between ninth grade and 12th grade is also two-thirds of those entering ninth grade. This means that out of every 10 children entering ninth grade, fewer than seven graduate. Then about four of the original 10 go on to college. As will be discussed in the next section, only about half of those entering college actually graduate, leaving only two persons of the original 10 who obtain a college degree.

Many educators (and business leaders) feel the world today demands more of high school graduates. The No Child Left Behind Act (NCLB) of 2002 aims at increasing the performance of high school graduates by starting with increased standard testing in elementary school in grades three through eight. Schools that fail to show improvement face sanctions, and parents can take their children out of underperforming schools and enroll them in better performing schools. President Bush now wants to expand the regular testing into high schools.

There are many debates about the effectiveness of the NCLB Act, but there are other pressures on high schools to offer an academic curriculum to every child, regardless of whether the student intends to go to college. Such plans are generally gaining favor across the country. Also, even though there are fierce debates about the issue in places like California, the concept of requiring high school graduates to take a graduation exam to prove they actually learned something in high school is growing. Years of such practices as "social promotion" or "automatic promotion" have resulted in high school graduates who are barely literate and basically unable to function in society, let alone find a decent job. Much pressure is being brought to end such practices so that in the future, a high school diploma will actually be an indication that the bearer did more in school than simply last long enough to graduate. For those opposed to social promotional and similar practices, the future is promising.

The Issue of Access versus Academics

There is an overriding issue in the debate over academic standards that is unique to the United States. Following the concept of public (free) school for all that was expressed in the 1954 desegregation decision, in 1975 an act of the federal government decreed a Free Appropriate Public Education (FAPE) for all handicapped or disabled children. The nature of these disabilities was primarily mental or emotional, not just physical. The definition of what constitutes a disability has continued to expand. Also, in 1982 the Supreme Court ruled that any person in the country, while here legally or not, must be provided with a free public education under the court's interpretation of the fourteenth amendment.

These rulings basically mean that the United States has provided access to a public elementary/secondary education to literally everyone of the proper age residing in the country. Census figures show that over 90 percent of school-age children are actually enrolled in school. The public schools thus carry the burden of providing this access while being under fire to maintain high academic standards. It is not clear if this combination of requirements can be met. Not every child in any country is capable of performing well at high school levels, but this is essentially the demand made upon public schools in the United States.

Much has been made of the comparisons of test scores between high school students in other countries and in the United States, with the United States ranking very low. But analyses of these comparisons have shown that the comparisons are not always apples-to-apples. For example, in 1983, reports on comparisons made in prior years showed that the United States did not fare well considering average scores on a number of tests. But test takers in the United States were drawn from a youth group where about 75 percent of all age-eligible youth were enrolled in high school. Similar ratios in Sweden were about 45–50 percent, and in Germany it was about 15 percent. This meant the average youth in the United States was competing against a relatively elite youth in other countries. If comparisons were made only among the elite of all test takers in the countries being compared (the top 5 and 10 percent), there were little if any differences in the test scores of the countries involved.

Thus, the tendency in the United States to show no cultural bias in determining who gets into high school essentially puts the United States at a disadvantage when comparing the average student in high school here to the average student in a more restrictive environment elsewhere. Thus, such comparisons must be made with great care. An example of this kind of problem is that school districts today point out that the new No Child Left Behind (NCLB) Act requires annual testing of students in third through eighth grades without "grouping" children along race and class lines to hide disparities that are known to exist. Using averages hides these gaps. In addition, schools would normally exclude "special education" (handicapped) children and limited English proficiency students from the test results — or even simply tell such students to stay home on test days. The new NCLB Act forbids such actions. The fact that school districts used such practices shows how difficult it is to properly compare average test results in a school system with a very diverse student body to those with a more homogeneous student body. Diversity and high academic achievement are not easily achieved simultaneously.

Also, the problem of ensuring that everyone who eventually graduates from high school in the United States has received and absorbed an education that is suitable for success in life after high school is greatly complicated by the incredibly diverse population in the nation's high schools. This brings us back to the problem of determining the most suitable curriculum for use in our high schools.

The words of Ernest L. Boyer, president of the Carnegie Foundation for the Advancement of Teaching at the time he wrote a book titled *High School*, published in 1983, are still true today: "What is taught in high school determines what is learned." Boyer favored a more rigorous academic curriculum in high school in his time, and that appears to be the direction that most favor today, in spite of the great diversity of the high school (and elementary school) population in the United States.

The Present College/University/Postsecondary Education System

In the present system, undergraduate "grades" are commonly known as the freshman, sophomore, junior, and senior grades. In a college or university, the equivalent of four successfully completed years result in a bachelor of arts (BA) or a bachelor of science (BS) degree, or sometimes a different bachelor's degree such as bachelor of fine arts (BFA).

In a community college, the completion of the "lower division" of two years results in an associate of arts (AA) degree. In some states only lower division programs are available and students must transfer to a four-year college or university to get a higher degree. Where an upper division school is available, two more years of school can produce a BA, BS, or BT (bachelor of technology) degree.

Postgraduate school requires another one to three years leading to a master of arts (MA), master of science (MS), master of education (MEd), or master of fine arts (MFA). After attaining the master's level, another three or more years can achieve degrees such as doctor of philosophy (PhD) or doctor of arts, doctor of education, or doctor of theology.

Professional doctorate degrees such as doctor of medicine, doctor of pharmacy, or juris doctor (law degree) sometimes require additional effort such as an internship in medicine or the passing of the bar exam in law before one is considered fully trained.

Public and private schools have a much different meaning in postsecondary education than they do in elementary and secondary education. To begin with, any college may award associate, bachelor, or master's degrees, but only the university can award the PhD, or doctorate degree. A typical university consists of undergraduate colleges awarding bachelor's degrees, and graduate schools awarding master's degrees and doctorates. Each state maintains its own public university system, which is always nonprofit (but is by no means free). Most areas will also have private institutions, which may or may not be nonprofit (but again are by no means free).

Private universities generally charge higher tuition than their state-supported public counterparts because they have no direct state support. But because of their state support, public universities charge much higher tuition to out-of-state students. Scholarships and similar aid is available in both types of schools. Private universities are generally considered of higher quality than public universities, but many exceptions exist. But because of the lack of the red tape often involved with state-supported schools, and the normal private versus public employment incentives, private universities almost always offer better customer services.

Tuition at state schools (for state residents) runs typically $15,000 per year, with many other fees and costs added on. At prestigious private schools tuition can run up to $40,000 yearly, although $20,000 to $40,000 is more typical. This is why so many students apply for federal student loans, which in turn is why the long hand of the government reaches into so many colleges and universities. Private or not, if one student in the school receives federal financial aid, the entire school is deemed to receive federal financial aid and thus must meet certain federal regulations (more about this in the next section).

There are well over 1,500 four-year colleges and universities in the United States, as well as over 1,000 community colleges. They range from the prestigious schools noted above, where only 10–15 percent of all applicants are admitted, to community colleges where essentially any member of the community can find admission. Their costs vary just as widely, and literally any person who wishes to go to college in the United States can find a way to do so. Countless scholarships and aid programs exist, and courses are offered at nights and on weekends so students can work and go to college at the same time. Many colleges even offer programs over the Internet so the student almost never needs to set foot on campus. Many community colleges offer an initial two-year program, after which a transfer to a four-year college is easily accomplished and only two years of higher costs are required to get a four-year degree. The permutations and combinations are endless.

If a student wishes to go to Harvard or Stanford, then a long, hard, and expensive road lies ahead (although highly qualified students can find many sources of aid from both schools). But if someone is simply determined to get a bachelor's degree in their field of choice, then that is possible for anyone — literally anyone — willing to make the disciplined attempt.

The Evolution of the Present College/University/ Postsecondary Education System

Unlike the slow and haphazard growth of elementary and secondary education in the United States, the new settlers immediately established college/university/postsecondary education. They felt such education was clearly necessary to create the leaders and ministers needed to direct the new country the settlers were building.

Harvard University was founded in 1636, nearly simultaneous with the arrival of the earliest settlers in Massachusetts and their establishment of new communities. The College of William and Mary in Virginia (where Thomas Jefferson would be educated) and Yale University in Connecticut followed near the turn of the century. Before the Revolutionary War in 1776, all of the universities that would become members of the prestigious Ivy League, except Cornell, were founded in the area between Pennsylvania and New England.

The number of colleges in the United States grew steadily into the 1800s, and when the Civil War broke out in 1861, the Congress took advantage of the absence of the southern legislators to pass the Morrill Land-Grant Act, a step that subsequently dramatically increased the number of colleges. The Morrill Act, in simplest form, gave 30,000 acres of government land to each state for each senator and representative the state had. These lands were to be used to build state universities (as opposed to the privately owned Ivy League schools), and income derived from the land grants and from the federal government would be used to operate the schools. The schools were intended for the nonelite and would offer education in such nonclassical subjects as agriculture and engineering.

The number of colleges and universities exploded after the passage of the Morrill Act. Many subsequent amendments and expansions of the act would be forthcoming in future years. The act would also help in the building of black colleges after the Civil War ended in 1865. There are now 105 land-grant institutions in the nation, including at least one in every state and territory. There were more than 150 new colleges and universities built in the United States between 1880 and 1885, an average of more than 30 per year. But there were forces other than the Morrill Act involved in this building boom, although it played a very important part.

After the Civil War ended, there was an impressive effort to build black colleges for the adult portion of the four million newly freed slaves who needed education to be able to become self-sufficient. The so-called federal Freedmen's Bureau, formed in 1865, was a great help in getting this effort started, and although southern "Black Codes" kept these schools segregated, the hunger for education rapidly resulted in the creation of a number of black colleges.

Also, after Oberlin College in Ohio opened in 1833 and by 1837 was admitting women on the same basis as men, there was a new emphasis in the movement to permit women to obtain a college education, an unthinkable thought before this time. Oberlin later was one of the first colleges to admit blacks, and thus it became a key player in the two discrimination issues that affected colleges and universities in their history of growth in the United States — racial discrimination and gender discrimination. As it turned out, gender discrimination became a more intractable item than racial discrimination at the postsecondary educational level.

Racial Discrimination at the Postsecondary Education Level

To a large extent, racial discrimination at the postsecondary level tracked the history of such discrimination at the elementary/secondary level. The effect was strongest in the South, but generally in other parts of the country integration was easier in colleges and universities than at the elementary/secondary level.

The National Association for the Advancement of Colored People

(NAACP), as described briefly in the previous section, had begun to chip away at segregation in southern colleges by focusing on graduate schools, especially law schools. Their reasoning was that the judges who heard their cases, law school graduates themselves, would be most sympathetic to and most cognizant of the claims of the NAACP that blacks were not receiving an equal education, even if "separate but equal" was a legitimate concept.

In case after case through the 1930s and 1940s, the NAACP was easily able to show that blacks in southern law schools, who were shunted to the basements of decrepit downtown buildings or forced to stay behind roped-off areas in law schools and forced to eat lunch or use libraries at different times than whites, were not receiving "separate but equal" educations. A number of southern schools were uneasily considering some sort of integration as a better alternative to the cost of building truly equal schools, when the 1954 Supreme Court ruling declared the "separate but equal" concept unconstitutional.

There were riots at the University of Alabama in 1956 (Autherine Lucy) and at the University of Mississippi in 1962 (James Meredith) when blacks attempted to attend school there, but the South slowly accepted the idea of integration at the college level. James Meredith graduated from the University of Mississippi in 1963. This acceptance was helped at some major schools when the coaches of their top-flight football and basketball programs said they could no longer compete nationally without recruiting black athletes. Integration in the South was also given a boost when the prestigious University of Virginia reluctantly accepted limited integration shortly before the 1954 Supreme Court ruling (however, on another front, the school did not become fully coeducational until 1970).

To a large extent, the battle over racial discrimination in colleges and universities has evolved into a battle over affirmative action, and the cycle has been essentially reversed today in that colleges want to do more in the name of affirmative action that the courts will necessarily allow. In 1978 the Supreme Court threw out the use of quotas in college admission practices in a suit brought by Alan Bakke, who was denied admission to medical school to make room for less qualified minorities to meet the minority quota goals of the University of California at Davis. The Court ruled somewhat vaguely that race could be one of several factors in determining admission policies in the interest of maintaining a diverse student body, but quotas per se were unconstitutional.

However, in 1996 the Supreme Court let stand a ruling by the fifth Circuit Court of Appeals that the magic word "diverse" had no legal standing, and that "educational diversity" was not recognized as a compelling state interest and therefore not a reason for affirmative actions that permitted less-qualified minority students to displace more-qualified nonminority students (the decision was known as the Hopwood case). A few years later the states of California, Washington, and Florida passed laws that banned the use of race in determining admission to college as well as in other areas of state business. Affirmative action seemed on the way out.

But in 2003 the Supreme Court reversed itself and decided a "diverse" student body was a compelling state interest in a case involving graduate admissions at the University of Michigan law school. The vote was 5–4, as it often is in cases of this type, and the next legal view of the merits of a diverse student body may well depend on what a given jurist had for breakfast the morning before the case was argued.

This is actually a very minor issue today, however passionate colleges may be in arguing that they want a diverse student body, and however passionate would-be students may be in arguing that they should not be displaced by a less-qualified minority student in the interest of a concept as arcane as a diverse student body. There are even studies showing that affirmative action does a disservice to minorities who are admitted to a school they are not qualified for and who then drop out once they find themselves hopelessly over their heads. The result is fewer minority lawyers, for example, rather than more. The reason it is a minor issue is because only very competitive schools unable to accept all qualified students who apply get involved in this issue.

These schools are a relative handful among the over 1,500 colleges in the United States, and the number of students involved is similarly small. The key point of interest is that the colleges are pressing the case against the courts (and often their legislatures) to find ways to take race into account in a way favorable to minorities in the admission of students. There are few, if any, cases where an otherwise qualified individual is denied the opportunity for an education due to race. In that sense, racial discrimination at the postsecondary level of education was eliminated in the United States by the end of the twentieth century.

Gender Discrimination at the Postsecondary Education Level

Although gender discrimination in elementary and secondary education has been almost nonexistent in the United States, it has been a major problem at the postsecondary level until almost exactly at the end of the twentieth century. Elementary and secondary education had no gender problem initially, primarily because communities could not afford to build separate schools for girls and boys, and thus they attended school together until well into their teens. While high schools were developing in the 1800s, there were some gender issues about whether girls should attend, but these issues were soon washed away in the flood of children of high school age needing to be educated. Girls once again attended with boys.

But at the postsecondary level, it was originally unheard of for women to go to college. It took almost 250 years for Harvard to become a fully coeducational school after its founding in 1636. Women were considered a "protected" group and college was beyond them. A president of Harvard in 1873 was quoted as saying that if women went to college, their blood flow would be diverted to their brains from their uteruses, and great harm would be done to their childbearing abilities. Even as colleges for women became a reality in the later 1800s, it was said no buildings on campus for women should be higher than two stories because a woman could not be expected to climb more than one floor above ground level without harming herself and her reproductive capabilities.

Those who struggled to win the right to vote for women in 1920 probably heard many stories like this, but they seem unbelievably quaint today. In 1833 Oberlin College was founded in Ohio, and even though it intended to admit women at its founding (its first student body of 44 students included 15 women), it took until 1837 before women were admitted on the same basis and could take the same courses as men. Also, in 1837, the institution that would become Mount Holyoke was founded in Massachusetts as the first institution of higher learning in the United States that was intended only for women. After the ice was broken, more existing colleges slowly began to admit women, and colleges specifically for women only began to be built in substantial numbers.

"Practical" reasons helped women in their attempts to enroll in existing colleges as the later 1800s progressed. Many colleges had budget problems, and when administrators discovered that the money they received as tuition and fees from women spent just as well as money received from men, the administrators were happy to make their colleges coeducational. There were student revolts by men in some previous all-male colleges over such conversions, but these generally passed without much lasting effect. Ironically, about a century later, when some previously all-women colleges wanted to become coeducational for similar financial reasons, it was the turn of the women students to rebel.

The time after the Civil War saw a great building boom in colleges for women only as part of the overall boom in colleges in general. This boom was triggered by the Morrill Land-Grant Act. Many black colleges were also built in this period. This book's chronology lists many of the colleges built in this period that were of some significance. Only a relative few of the many colleges built are noted, but many of those that broke new ground in some way are listed.

As an example of how deeply ingrained gender bias was in this era, Lincoln University was founded for blacks in 1854 just above the Mason-Dixon line in southeastern Pennsylvania, where it could get started even before the Civil War. The college was a beacon of education for blacks, and it graduated 20 percent of black physicians and 10 percent of black lawyers in the entire United States during the first 100 years after it was founded. But nearly every one of those 100 years passed before Lincoln University finally became coeducational in 1952.

Between 1865 and 1893, the "Seven Sisters," a prestigious group of women's colleges that considered themselves equivalent to the Ivy League colleges in educational quality, were founded. Mount Holyoke was founded first in 1837, but it did not officially become a college until 1888. The Seven Sisters formally became loosely associated in 1927, and their theme was that they offered a "separate but equal" education for women that was every bit as good as that offered by the Ivy League schools. The Ivy League schools did not accept women as undergraduates (except for Cornell, which wasn't opened for business until 1868). The sense of the meeting in 1927 was that these schools for women were not really interested in having women attend Ivy League schools, thank you very much, because in many ways the education a woman could receive at an all-woman school was superior to that received at a coeducational school.

The question of gender bias finally ended legally in 1972 when Title IX, an amendment to the Higher Education Act, banned gender discrimination by federally funded institutions. As noted before, the term "federally funded institution" became essentially universal when the Supreme Court in 1984 defined any institution with any student receiving federal aid in the form of a student loan as basically a "federally funded institution." The Supreme Court ruling initially was applied to rather narrow portions of the school, but Congress in 1988 broadened the application to the whole school. A huge number of colleges receive federally funded research and study contracts and thus would have fallen under the definition of receiving government aid anyhow, but today it is very hard, if not impossible, for any college in the United States to demonstrate that it is not the recipient of "federal aid" in some way.

The Title IX Amendment of 1972 was planned not to take effect until 1977, but colleges and universities realized what was coming in terms of admission policies, and all schools rapidly joined the coeducational bandwagon. Besides, by the end of the 1960s few schools could say with a straight face that men and women should not be treated alike in terms of attending college. A symbolic event took place in 1969 when Yale University, a bastion for men for the prior 268 years, and Vassar College, a leading school for women for 105 years, both became fully coeducational.

Some developments flowed from Title IX that were unexpected when it was initiated in 1972. One was that women would extend coeducational status even to previously all-male state military schools. At the federal level, the U.S. Military Academy at West Point, the Naval Academy, and the Air Force Academy became coeducational in 1976. But determined women also forced the Citadel in South Carolina, in 1993, and the Virginia Military Institute (VMI), in 1996, to become coeducational. Various "separate but equal" plans were proposed to maintain an all-male part of VMI, but the Supreme Court ruled that in these times gender-based classifications were acceptable only in extraordinary circumstances.

VMI considered becoming a private institution rather than a coeducational public school, but avoiding any federal aid at all would have been too complicated and expensive. Once again financial considerations overcame long-held philosophical considerations. As VMI became coeducational, the United States military also became coeducational in its various officer-training establishments. The long tradition of all-male public military institutions in the United States ended just as the twentieth century was coming to a close.

Another unexpected development of Title IX was its impact on sports. As physical education was considered part of the educational process in college (and also in elementary and secondary school), lawsuits began to arise claiming the physical facilities and other parts of physical education provided for women was definitely not equal to that provided for men, and thus was a violation of Title IX. The remedies for this problem quickly evolved into a determination of whether the funds expended for women and men's sports were equal in proportion to the number of women and men students (the issue also became prevalent in high schools).

But the hopes of women for greatly expanded opportunities in sports were often not realized as budget-strapped colleges simply cut the number of men's sports to bring the ratio of spending into balance. Men were understandably unhappy with this solution and began to file lawsuits of their own. In some ways it seems ironic that the great issue of gender equity in education would come down to a question of which gender has the most attractive and/or best equipped locker rooms. But few people can anticipate what directions fundamental changes in such things as gender equity can take.

This particular problem may be with us for a long time, because there are other forces, primarily financial, at play in college sports besides the question of gender equity. The idealized "student athlete" playing sports as part of his (or her) general education is a myth at many large schools. It may still apply in the Ivy League, which greatly limits the conditions covering athletic scholarships, but at schools which are nationally prominent in football or basketball (and other sports at very large schools), sports have become a moneymaking business that contributes directly to the school budget and also prompts higher alumni contributions. The amounts of money involved are very large.

The new "student athlete" is often a student who could barely make it through high school, whose grades often do not represent actual performance there, and whose "studies" at college include the old clichés of basketweaving and or advanced partying. There recently was an incident at the University of Georgia where basketball players were given a course that included a test with questions such as how many points are given for a three-point basket. Critics joked that the problem was not so much that questions such as this were asked, but that players still could not pass the test.

Even college presidents have been involved in efforts to transfer "students" from other schools who have no prospects of gaining an education, but who could possibly contribute to a winning sports team. These "students" are "paid" with a scholarship that covers the expenses of their college education, but in many places few actually graduate when their eligibility for playing sports is over. This is a sort of fraud, and the National Collegiate Athletic Association (NCAA) is constantly trying to tighten recruiting practices and place sanctions on schools whose student athletes fail to graduate at a certain rate. But many of these students are poor blacks, and restrictions on their ability to win an athletic scholarship are considered by some to be racial discrimination on the basis that they had no control over the poor education they received in an inner-city high school, and their only hope of advancement was a college scholarship hopefully leading to a position in professional sports, even if not a degree.

This issue is basically beyond the scope of this book, but it needs to be recognized that Title IX does not operate in a vacuum. The majority of colleges do not operate sports programs for a profit with essentially "hired guns," and they accommodate well to Title IX. But where athletics has become a business, Title IX problems occur and will continue to occur. In many cases, the football program pays the budget for all other sports. As no one yet wants to see (or pay to see) college women play football, administrators are incensed at being forced to pay for women's sports when they make no contribution to the budget. However, at some schools women's basketball has become very popular (and profitable), bringing along with it the same kind of recruiting fraud as occurs in men's sports. It is a very complicated problem, and as such will probably continue to be with us for a long time.

The major accomplishments of postsecondary education in the twentieth century were the elimination of racial bias and the elimination, at least in admission policy, of gender bias. The result has been what some call the "feminization" of the college experience. More girls than boys now graduate from high school (and with more honors), and more girls than boys, accordingly, go on to college. Women now account for 60 percent of the enrolled undergraduate population. Also, women earned 58 percent of the bachelor's degrees awarded in the United States in the 2003–04 school year, a trend that started in 1989–90 when more women than men earned bachelor's degrees for the first time ever. In 1949–50, men earned 75 percent of the bachelor's degrees. This trend is expected to continue. In an election, a "winning" margin of 58 percent would be considered a landslide.

Some say the gap is generally limited to lower-income students and minorities, where women tend to go on to college while the men in that population tend to go to work or to the military. Others say the gap crosses race and class lines. More men than women tend to go to schools emphasizing engineering, science, or business, and such prestigious schools as Stanford and those in the Ivy League enroll more men than women. But the highly sought-after University of California at Berkeley campus enrolls 26 percent of female freshman applicants compared to 22 percent of males. Also, women outnumbered men among medical school applicants in 2004 for the second straight year, and more women than men now earn doctorates of all types.

No matter how the data are sliced and diced, women have made huge strides in a relatively short time in gaining the edge in a college population that in many places used to refuse to admit them on equal terms with men. There are still some colleges that stay for women only because they feel women get a better education in a women-only atmosphere. The legal status of such schools may be on shaky ground, but if no males are agitating for entry, the issue may never come up. Based on the history of women to agitate for entry where they were previously refused due to gender, it is hard to imagine there are many all-male schools left in the United States (at least none of interest to women).

The Role of the Federal Government in Education in the United States

Unlike the educational systems of many other countries, the educational system in the United States is highly decentralized. The individual states are responsible for education, and the federal government plays no direct role in determining curriculum or educational standards. The primary role of the federal government is to administer funding programs involving education and to enforce federal education laws involved with privacy and civil rights. The quality of education is maintained through a relatively informal "accreditation" process over which the federal government has no direct control.

The original constitution of the United States makes no mention of education. This right was jealously guarded by the states to the extent that when a federal Department of Education was created in 1867, it was quickly demoted to an "office" in 1868 after the states complained. More than a century later, when President Jimmy Carter created a new Department of Education in 1979, there were many complaints again. A large number of Republicans saw the department as an unwanted federal bureaucratic intrusion into state and local control of schools. During the 1980s there were calls for abolition of the department, but several Republican administrations declined to implement the idea. By the 1990s there was bipartisan support for the department, which continues to function today.

The Department of Education has the following operating units:

- Office of Federal Student Aid
- Office for Civil Rights
- Office of Educational Research and Improvement
- Office of Elementary and Secondary Education
- Office of English Language Acquisition, Language Enhancement and Academic Achievement for Limited English Proficient Students
- Office of Postsecondary Education
- Office of Special Education and Rehabilitation Services
- Office of Vocational and Adult Education

Probably the most important federal act in terms of how it impacted education at the state level was the Elementary and Secondary Education Act (ESEA) of 1965. It had many subsequent amendments in the process of being reauthorized over the years, and it essentially was rewritten into the No Child Left Behind (NCLB) Act of 2001 that was signed by President Bush in early 2002. ESEA was essentially an act of redress in that it was based on the assumption that poor and minority children were being hampered in their climb out of poverty by the lack of the extra education they needed to overcome their undesirable start in life, and federal funds were funneled in their direction (administered by the states) to help overcome their basic educational deficiencies. NCLB expands federal oversight of schools and focuses on sequential academic testing of schoolchildren to be sure they are advancing, and provides sanctions for schools perceived to be failing in their educational mission. It is controversial, as is every federal step into the educational process, and it almost surely will continue to be controversial as it evolves in future years.

Key postsecondary acts have usually been less controversial because they generally clearly have dealt with funding issues, and, as some have noted, the population they deal with are generally adults largely unencumbered by the degree of emotional intensity parents bring to elementary/secondary school decisions. Notable postsecondary acts include the Servicemen's Readjustment Act of 1944 (the "GI Bill") and the Higher Education Act of 1965. Both acts were subsequently amended in later years to provide even more benefits.

The GI Bill was responsible for a great influx of students into the nation's colleges, to the extent that many colleges underwent building booms to handle the traffic. The GIs came from all walks of life and in all colors, and their massive movement into college permanently broke whatever vestiges were left of the idea that a college education was primarily for the elite. In many ways it helped trigger a great economic boom into the 1950s instead of the depression many feared would follow the return of the armed forces from World War II.

The Higher Education Act of 1965 focused on financial aid to colleges and student loans for the students attending college. Few students attend college today without the assistance of a student loan. It was the amendments to the act in 1972 that underlined the concept of gender equality and that ultimately created the Title IX controversy in college sports. This was a perfect example of the concept that when one accepts a loan of money, one also accepts the conditions that come with it, especially if the loan is from a government entity.

None of the acts addressed such volatile issues as desegregation, or the rights of the handicapped to a free public education, or the rights of illegal immigrants to a free public education. Similarly, they do not address such issues as freedom of (or from) religion in schools. This is because such issues do not usually arise from legislation, but rather from court rulings. Court rulings of all types have dramatically affected the educational process in the United States. Basically, the prime effect of the federal government on education in the United States arises from the rulings of the judicial branch of government. Many examples of such rulings are listed in the chronology.

To best understand how this process has evolved, it is necessary to review the manner in which the courts in the United States essentially end up writing the laws of the country. It is also necessary to review the constitutional issues on which the highest court, the United States Supreme Court, bases its decisions. The Supreme Court basically does not consider "cases of fact." Those are determined by lower courts. The Supreme Court considers primarily only those cases that appear to need a decision based on the interpretation of a "constitutional issue," or some body of legislation such as the civil rights acts.

The Evolving Role of the Courts in the Establishment of Laws

For a long time in the early history of the United States, courts made rulings where no specific law existed for a given situation. They were guided by custom and decisions that had built up over time, a body of knowledge known as "common law." This system was a direct inheritance from England, and common law still affects our world today, even if to a much lesser extent than it once did.

Although legislatures at all levels write countless statues today, only if the case of A versus B falls exactly within the parameters of the statue does the law apply as written. But if the case of C versus D varies slightly from what is written in the statue, the judge handling the case essentially writes a modified law when he or she decides if the statue applies to the new case, and, if so, who has the winning position. This new law will be used as a precedent for subsequent cases of the C versus D type. Precedent is extremely important, because by knowing that the judge will give it great weight, people planning various decisions have a basis for knowing what the legalities of their new decision will likely be. Precedent is not just an easy way out for the next ruling judge; it prevents chaos in that it keeps a body of law up to date. The first judge to rule on cases of the C versus D type thus writes the law for all new cases of that type.

Now we come to an E versus F case that differs slightly from all prior cases. Another judge writes another new law, and so on and so forth. The original statue may be obsolete in practice, but a new body of law has evolved, all written by the courts. Anyone familiar with the incredibly complex tax code used by the IRS knows that much of that tax code was created using the process just described.

In a country like the United States, where the "rule of law" applies, and there is no "Supreme Ruler" whose word is law, every person has the opportunity to apply for redress in the courts if a new law is passed that the person finds unfair or unjust in his or her opinion, or if a new law that would help the person is not being properly administered. This greatly assists the concept that the courts write the laws because there is no end of incoming actions that need to be decided against existing statutes. The courts must decide if a statute applies to the case in question, or if a new ruling must be made that would change the nature of the statute.

The courts in each state initially act to decide the case, but in a nation of laws such as ours, seemingly endless appeals can be made. Thus, the case may reach the Supreme Court of the given state, and then move on to one of the 11 United States Circuit Courts that cover various areas of the nation. The final appeal is to the Supreme Court of the United States. However, as noted before, the Supreme Court does not accept cases that it considers to require "only" a "finding of fact." Cases of that type are left to the lower courts. If the Supreme Court feels that a constitutional question is being raised, or that the case concerns an issue of national significance that applies widely and requires a definitive decision of some sort, then the Supreme Court may take the case. The Supreme Court basically accepts very few cases for review, but these are usually the cases that are of great interest in the country, and that accordingly will have a great impact.

Considering the fact discussed earlier in this introduction that one in four people in the country are involved in the education process, it is not unexpected that a great number of issues dealing with education reach the Supreme Court. In fact, considering that anyone who takes issue with a new or existing law can try to sue for redress in the courts, the number of education cases reaching the Supreme Court is actually surprisingly small.

The conclusion is that most notable crises in education occur as a result of court decisions, and these cases often rise to the level of requiring an interpretation of a constitutional matter. The constitutional basis on which most of these laws are decided is discussed in the next section.

The Constitutional Issues Most Often Applied to Education Cases

The First Amendment to the Constitution, which was part of the Bill of Rights required to be written to get the states to agree to the first Constitution, raises issues that are often cited in education cases. The amendment reads: "Congress shall make no law respecting an establishment of religion, or prohibiting the free exercise thereof; or abridging the freedom of speech, or of the press; or the right of the people peacefully to assemble, and to petition the government for a redress of grievances."

The "establishment clause" of the First Amendment is the basis for most cases objecting to religious practices as they affect schools. Considering that the initial curriculum of "common schools" in the early history of the country consisted of the "four Rs" (religion, reading, writing, and arithmetic), the religious issue has been with us for a long time. The Supreme Court has generally been very firm in eliminating such school practices as beginning the day with required prayers or Bible readings. These issues are relatively easy to decide, even if the decisions caused great emotional outpourings on both sides of the issue, and still do.

But a question such as whether a poster showing the Ten Commandments in a teacher's office is acceptable, or whether a student body decision to include a prayer read by a student at a commencement exercise is permissible, or the question of whether the local Hindu society can use school facilities after hours for essentially secular meetings, is not so easily decided. The decision often depends on the exact circumstances involved. If one carefully reads the decisions of the Supreme Court in this and other areas (many are listed in the chronology), one cannot help but be impressed by the great care the justices take to make an appropriate decision.

The part of the First Amendment that addresses "abridging freedom of speech, or of the press" has become especially complex in present times. It is hard to imagine that the founding fathers who wrote the Bill of Rights ever imagined that such things as burning the flag, or the length of a skirt worn to school by a girl, or the length of hair worn by a boy would become "free speech" issues. In this area, one would have to conclude that the Supreme Court has generally bent over backwards to protect freedom of speech in this country, even in situations that seem to use the protection of the free speech amendment in an almost trivial way. However, the Supreme Court has consistently ruled that even though the protection is often being sought in a very unusual manner, the importance of free speech in the country usually trumps other considerations.

The Fifth Amendment is known for its use in criminal cases against self-incrimination and the "double jeopardy" concept forbidding trying the same person twice for the same offense. However, the last sentence of the Fifth Amendment reads that no one can "be deprived of life, liberty, or property, without due process of law." The "due process clause" often arises in education cases where a teacher or coach claims to have been unfairly fired from a job or unfairly prevented from taking certain actions. This clause does not appear in decisions nearly as often as the First Amendment, but the due process clause, like the free speech clause, can often be used in very imaginative ways when persons are seeking redress for a perceived injury.

Aside from the articles listed in the Bill of Rights, the next amendment that is frequently cited in education cases is the Fourteenth Amendment. This amendment was written in 1866 and ratified in 1868. The amendment was basically written in response to the perceived unfair and unjust treatment former slaves were receiving in the southern states following the end of the Civil War. The southern states were required to agree to the Fourteenth Amendment as a condition of being readmitted into the Union. Many southern states declined to do so, but the question became moot when enough other states ratified the amendment and thus made it part of the Constitution.

Many southern states greatly diluted the effect of the amendment by passing state laws to make it hard for the amendment to be fully implemented, and the Supreme Court in the so-called 1873 Slaughterhouse Cases permitted many of these state actions. But these issues have generally faded into the past.

A Supreme Court decision that did not fade away and that essentially setup the famous desegregation ruling of 1954 was the *Plessy* decision of 1896. In this case the Supreme Court established the "separate but equal" concept as the law of the land by ruling against a black man who had appealed a Louisiana law requiring him to ride in a different railway passenger car than whites. Even 30 years after the end of the Civil War, Justice Henry Brown issued a ruling essentially saying that the intention of the Fourteenth Amendment granted Plessy the right he was seeking, but Brown felt "social" equality or "commingling" of the races "could not" have been intended.

The Plessy ruling was primarily the basis Southern states used to create segregated schools (and a segregated culture). But the "separate but equal" concept slowly fell apart over the years as the National Association for the Advancement of Colored People (NAACP), founded in 1909, showed that the black side of the equation was not remotely equal in schools at any level. The Supreme Court felt greater and greater pressure to overturn the Plessy decision, an action the Supreme Court has never taken lightly. But the Supreme Court did so in May 1954.

The language in the Fourteenth Amendment that was cited in 1954 and in many subsequent education cases is that no state shall deprive "any person of life, liberty, or property, without due process of law; or deny to any person within its jurisdiction the equal protection of the laws." The words "equal protection of the laws" were the key to the 1954 desegregation decision. The Court ruled that "separate" is inherently unequal in public education because "intangible" issues have a detrimental effect on minority children in that such separation is interpreted as a sign of inferiority. The "flavor" of this concept was used by the Court to give "great scrutiny" to attempts by state military colleges to avoid admitting females by the use of "separate but equal" college programs in the 1990s. The result of the great scrutiny was that in "present times" such exclusion by gender could no longer stand.

Now that we have a brief understanding of how the courts actually write the majority of the body of laws concerning education, and also have some understanding of the basis used for the writing of such laws, we can review the major laws and court decisions of the twentieth century based on the impact they had on the educational process in the United States.

The Major Laws and Court Decisions Impacting Education in the United States

1. The law or court decision having the biggest impact on education in the United States during the twentieth century was the decision of the United States Supreme Court in May 1954 banning school segregation on the basis of race. This was a two-part decision, with the 1954 ruling being followed by a May 1955 ruling intended to specify the manner in which remedies should be applied to the problems identified in 1954. The 1954 ruling became known as "Brown I," after the name of the case under which a

total of five cases were consolidated for consideration by the Court. Realizing the huge impact Brown I would have on the nation, the Court decided to take what stretched out to be a year before making recommendations on remedies. The 1955 decision became known as Brown II.

The Brown I decision was relatively clear and to the point, and was recognized as a decision that would change education in a major way in the United States. Unfortunately, the Brown II decision was quite ambiguous, and as a result it led to great problems. Brown I made it clear that integration of schools was now the law of the land. The District of Columbia and some border states began immediately to desegregate their schools. By the fall of 1954, 150 school districts in eight states had been integrated. The task clearly could be accomplished where people were working in a good-faith effort to make it happen. But state legislatures in Alabama, Georgia, Mississippi, South Carolina, and Virginia adopted resolutions of "interpolation and nullification" that declared the Court's decision to be null, void, and of no effect. Brown II needed to address such problems, but it failed to do so.

Brown II essentially said desegregation required varied local solutions. Local school districts and the local courts that originally heard desegregation cases should work together to implement Brown I with "all deliberate speed." This phrase became infamous. The states that strongly opposed integration seized upon the phrase to delay the process as long as possible. If one was determined to avoid integration, a period of several decades could readily be defined as meeting the requirement of "all deliberate speed."

Ironically, the school board in Little Rock, Arkansas, the city that was to become the poster child around the world for delay, riots, and the use of federal troops to enforce integration, actually made a good-faith plan to begin the process in the fall of 1957. But with the election in the fall of 1956 of Governor Orval Faubus, a dedicated segregationist, the plans of the school board were overwhelmed by anti-integration activity in the fall of 1957, and the well-known riots and dueling court filings ensued.

The Supreme Court issued a ruling in 1974 that went far to calm the troubled waters that had been created by local courts trying to enforce racial balance by busing. The Court ruled that achieving desegregation did not require "any particular racial balance in each school, grade, or classroom." The Court added that solutions of any kind must recognize the importance of local control over the operation of schools.

Integration finally was fully accomplished by the end of the century at all school levels, but de facto segregation exists today in many large cities (although not illegally as noted in the ruling above). Minorities primarily populate the inner-city schools, and most suburban schools are primarily populated by whites. This is a result of "white flight" from the inner cities. But in Los Angeles the nation's second-largest school district, the once black-white issue has changed dramatically. In Los Angeles the school population is 73 percent Hispanic, 12 percent black, 9 percent white, and 6 percent Asian. Most school racial issues occur between the black and Hispanic populations. No one is forbidden to enroll in any school anywhere based on race, but all racial issues have not disappeared.

The desegregation decision of 1954 still ranks as the decision most affecting education in the twentieth century. But 50 years after that decision, racial problems still affect schools, although the nature of the problems has changed greatly.

2. The Elementary and Secondary Education Act (ESEA) of 1965 was part of President Johnson's War on Poverty program. The act essentially focused on federal assistance to schools in low-income areas on the basis of redress. The act took the position that these areas required more educational services than more affluent areas, and the Act would supply the funds to provide these services. The act was politically strategic in that it specifically offered aid to poor children everywhere, cutting across racial and religious lines. This act has been substantially modified many times in the process of being reauthorized by subsequent administrations. It has slowly offered more aid for more items, increasing both the size and scope of the act and slowly involving the federal government more actively in school affairs. Its most recent version is the No Child Left Behind (NCLB) Act signed by President Bush in early 2002.

Constant contention surfaces when this act and its descendents are debated in Congress. Proponents support the funds disbursed to schools, while opponents attack provisions they consider to be unlawful federal government intrusion into education. As with any act or law providing funds, there are always "strings" attached that permit the federal government to at least influence certain elements of schooling. Opponents do not want to give up the much-needed funds, but want to spend them as they see fit. It's a cycle never likely to end. Schools constantly need more funds, and disbursers of funds, be they governmental or not, always want some control over how the funds are used.

3. The Higher Education Act of 1965 also addressed the issue of federal funds to support education. But this act was aimed at postsecondary colleges and universities, and its most significant outcome was the establishment of student loans. Very few students attend college today without making use of these loans. As usual, the loans are provided with attached stipulations that must be accepted by the institutions.

In 1972, an amendment to this act required schools receiving such funds to prohibit discrimination in educational opportunities on the basis of gender. The Title IX amendment led to an unexpected battle about the seem-ingly trivial question of whether sport teams for women were receiving funds equal in proportion to those provided to men. This battle continues today, as described in the gender discrimination section of this introduction.

4. States generally use property taxes as their primary method of fund-ing schools. In 1973 a lawsuit was filed in San Antonio, Texas, claiming that children, especially minority children, were receiving an inferior education because they lived in poor areas where property taxes were much lower than they were in affluent areas. The suit claimed violation of the equal protec-tion clause of the Fourteenth Amendment.

The Supreme Court ruled, first, that there is no fundamental right to education in the federal constitution. And second, that the Texas system did not discriminate against all poor people in Texas. The Court said the fund-ing scheme was "not so irrational as to be invidiously discriminatory." Jus-tice Lewis Powell noted that on the question of wealth and education, "the Equal Protection Clause does not require absolute equity or precisely equal advantages."

This ruling appeared to settle what had been a vexing question in other states, but the state of California took another tack and ruled that such inequities in funding did violate the constitution of California, if not the constitution of the United States. Accordingly, the state implemented an extremely complicated method of disbursing funds to schools in an attempt to achieve parity in per-child funding in all areas, regardless of the tax base in each area. Despite good intentions, California went from near the top in per-child funding in the nation to near the bottom. A property tax revolt followed, and funding of schools became primarily a state issue rather than a local one. Anyone looking at the general educational experience in inner-city schools in California compared to that in the affluent suburbs would be hard pressed to see how the "new" model of financing in practice is superior to the old.

5. In 1975 the Education for all Handicapped Children Act (EHA) was established. The act has been amended many times and is now known as the Individuals with Disabilities Education Act (IDEA). It has been defended in court as being required by the equal protection clause of the Fourteenth Amendment. The act requires that public schools provide a Free Appropri-ate Public Education (FAPE) for all handicapped/disabled children, from toddlers through college age. Federal aid is supplied as required, with the usual strings attached. The act greatly expanded access to schools for every-one by permitting or requiring handicapped children to attend regular schools, requiring many millions to be spent in supplying facilities and

specially trained teaching staffs. The definition of children eligible for assistance under the act has steadily increased, and over six million children are now covered by the act.

6. Part of the essential revolution in the relationship between the federal government and education that took place in the 1960s, when President Johnson had huge majorities in Congress and could pass nearly any bill he wished, was the notion of "affirmative action." The concept as Johnson defined it was that it was not enough to remove the longtime shackles that had prevented minorities from taking advantage of educational and other opportunities, it was necessary to give them some "special assistance" to obtain the full benefits of these opportunities. Hence, minorities were to be considered a little more equal than other groups to make up for past discrimination.

The court decision that most dramatically affected affirmative action as it applied to education was the Bakke decision of 1978. Alan Bakke sued the University of California because he was turned down twice when applying for medical school because the school had reserved quotas for minority applicants who were less qualified in the name of affirmative action. Bakke's suit claimed the state of California was in violation of both the Fourteenth Amendment and of the Civil Rights Act of 1964.

The Supreme Court ruled that strict quotas were definitely a violation of the civil rights law, but that the use of race as one criterion among several when considering admission to a school of higher education was constitutionally permissible. Bakke was ordered admitted to medical school, and quotas, used by many groups to avoid being sued under affirmative-action laws, were banned.

This "something for everyone" decision was an example of the Court bending over backwards to achieve consensus, but subsequent cases of this type more firmly barred a number of affirmative-action policies. Near the end of the century, several states barred the use of race in determining many administrative issues, including college admission. In a reversal of a previous decision upholding a ruling by a lower court stating that the desire to achieve a "diverse" student body had no legal standing, the Supreme Court in 2003 permitted some racial criteria to be used in admissions in the interest of achieving a "diverse student body," thus leaving the term somewhat in limbo. But except for colleges that felt diversity was important, policies to achieve affirmative action were greatly diminished early in the new century.

7. In a ruling that has greatly increased educational costs in states with many illegal immigrants, while expanding school access (a combination that often goes together), in 1982 the Supreme Court ruled in a Texas case that

illegal immigrants must receive a free public education as do other children in the state. The Court ruled that although the illegal immigrants are not citizens, they are "people" and thus are afforded Fourteenth Amendment "equal protection under the law." Such immigrants usually require additional costs to provide them with special training to overcome their limited English proficiency. These students also contribute to lower average academic test scores, as noted above, due to their lack of proficiency in the English language.

Large bilingual education programs were established around these students, but by the 1990s such programs fell out of favor. This was because too many students were placed in a bilingual "cocoon" and ended up graduating with limited English proficiency, the one thing they needed most to get good jobs or to go on to college. States such as California in 1998 and Arizona in 2000 barred the use of bilingual education in favor of English immersion programs. The No Child Left Behind Act confirmed this approach by clearly preferring English immersion programs. The act dropped the word "bilingual" from the Department of Education office responsible for such programs and made the term "language acquisition" the key phrase.

8. In 1984 the Supreme Court made official the ability of the federal government to reach into the affairs of any college via the strings attached to federal funds. In the Grove City case, the Court ruled that Grove City College, a private coeducational liberal arts school that had worked hard to preserve its autonomy by consistently refusing to accept state and federal financial assistance, met the definition of "receiving federal assistance" because some of its students received Basic Educational Opportunity Grants (BEOGs).

The school was free to opt out of the student assistance program and thus avoid any federal entanglement, but otherwise it was "tarred" with the federal assistance brush. This decision showed that only those colleges which were private, completely free of other federal or state ties, and capable of funding their students' needs from their own resources, could escape federal mandates. Few colleges can meet these requirements.

The Grove City case was actually quite narrowly applied by the Supreme Court in terms of the school activities affected, but once the "camel got its nose under the tent" in terms of the definition of what constitutes the receipt of federal funds, Congress in 1988 required Title IX (and other civil rights issues) to be applied to all operations of any school "receiving federal funds."

9. In 1996 the Supreme Court completed the destruction of the "separate but equal" concept, and fully eliminated gender discrimination in public schools offering postsecondary education. In the Virginia Military

Institute (VMI) case, the Supreme Court overturned a lower court ruling that the attempt of VMI to create a separate but equal program for women offered "substantively comparable" educational benefits. The Supreme Court ruled that the separate program would not provide women the same over-all opportunities as men, and as there was no "exceedingly persuasive justification" for the gender-biased admissions policy, especially under the "heightened scrutiny" of such policies in present times, the VMI policy violated the equal protection clause of the Fourteenth Amendment and was therefore unconstitutional.

This ruling was essentially the final step in the twentieth century to confirm that gender discrimination in public postsecondary schools was no longer constitutional in the United States. It also marked the end of male-only military institutions that had existed since colonial times.

Rulings Related to Church-State Issues

The preceding list of nine crucial education-oriented court cases does not include any of the numerous cases concerning the "establishment" clause of the First Amendment relative to the question of the establishment of religion by the state in public schools. There were many such decisions, but none actually made much difference in the way schools operated, regardless of the high emotions on each side. In the 1950s, courts threw out religious-based actions basically directed by school administrators, such as prayer and/or bible reading, to begin the school day. Later more subtle issues were raised, such as prayer by outside parties at commencement ceremonies. The basic rule was that if school administrators were involved, the practice in question was disallowed, but if it was wholly secular, some actions could pass muster.

Two decisions that were made by lower courts and not challenged by the Supreme Court in 1993 (thus leaving lower court decisions to stand as current law) demonstrated the present status of the feelings of the Court on "establishment" issues near the end of the twentieth century. The first case involved the words "under God" in the Pledge of Allegiance. The Supreme Court essentially seemed to feel that these words had become secularized like crèches and such things at Christmas and let the phrase stand. But this ruling only applied to the district in which it was made, and other similar cases were sure to arise in the future.

Another case a week later involved prayer at graduation services that was both voted for and led by students and approved by the school as non-sectarian and nonproselytizing. The Supreme Court let stand the lower court ruling that such prayer was acceptable.

The reaction to the decision also revealed much about the status of the "church/state" issue in the present-day United States. A group called the American Center for Law and Justice (ACLJ), led by Pat Robertson, praised the decision and mailed a "special bulletin" to every school district in the United States explaining how to have prayer included in graduation and similar ceremonies. The American Civil Liberties Union (ACLU) criticized the decision, said the bulletin mailed by the ACLJ contained misleading information, and mailed a bulletin of its own. It is primarily the actions of special interest groups like the ACLJ and the ACLU that keep this issue alive, appearing in court systems around the country at any given time.

Summary

One prime historical issue in education in the twentieth century was access to a free public elementary and secondary education for everyone. This action included the antisegregation Supreme Court decision of 1954, the basic law of 1975 mandating free public education for handicapped children, and the 1982 Supreme Court decision mandating a free public education for the children of illegal immigrants. At the end of the twentieth century practically everyone in the country who was of elementary/secondary school age (and many younger than that) was in school somewhere. One result is that the number of female high school graduates is now higher than the number of male graduates, with minority girls playing a leading role.

A similar historical issue of access took place in postsecondary education in the United States in the twentieth century, with the elimination of racial bias in admissions in 1954 and the elimination of gender bias via a combination of new laws and court decisions. Similar to the results in high school, the number of females both entering and graduating from college has overtaken the number of males. Females presently account for 57 percent of four-year college graduates in the United States.

The prime remaining issues in education that carried over into the twenty first century were the question of the level at which academic standards should be set in high school (a matter of debate for more than a century), and the issue of gender equity in sports for males and females (something debated at every educational level). The gender equity issue may substantially affect the relatively new question of exactly what is a "student-athlete" and should "students" be "hired" to make athletic profits for schools?

One key ongoing issue that affects all levels of education is the matter of inequity in the quality of the elementary and secondary educations available in inner-city schools versus their suburban counterparts. The question is not one of overt discrimination per se, but rather a question of learning environments, teacher qualifications, and available school resources. The fact that most inner-city schools serve low-income minority students and suburban schools serve mainly white and Asian students overlays this issue. The poor performance of minority students in college, if they get there at all, is due to a large extent to the inferior quality of their prior education and preparation. There is no easy solution to this imbalance, and it remains as a key item to be addressed in the future.

Education in the United States faces many other difficult issues today, including inadequate budgets, the quality of teachers and the level of compensation they receive, the vestiges of affirmative action and bilingual education and much more. Even with many issues still to be resolved, there can be no question of the historical significance of hurdles overcome by the U.S. education system over the last century, the twentieth century and/or carried over into the twenty first century, as noted just above.

THE CHRONOLOGY

This chronology begins in the early 1600s. As described in the introduction, this was when the first truly permanent settlers arrived in what would become the United States. Immigrants, primarily from Western Europe and Great Britain, settled along the Atlantic Coast, with different groups concentrated in the North, the mid–Atlantic territories, and the South. These groups established schools for their children following the customs of their places of origin, modifying these customs as they felt appropriate for their new homeland. Schools thus developed differently in each region. They followed new immigrants West while maintaining substantial differences in various regions consistent with the groups that founded them. It wasn't until the end of the Civil War in 1865 that schools began to develop in a relatively homogenous way across the United States.

Higher education at the college level, however, began to develop as soon as the new settlers arrived. There was general agreement that such education was needed for molding the future leaders of the new homeland. But while considerable differences existed in different parts of the country as to which children should attend elementary and secondary schools, what they should be taught, and at what ages they should begin and stop, the need for postsecondary colleges to teach elite males was considered self-apparent. Thus, colleges were established quickly and their number grew rapidly. The questions of who should attend college in terms of gender and race did not arise until many years later.

September 8, 1636— Harvard University was founded by a vote of the Great and General Court of the Massachusetts Bay Colony. Harvard is the oldest postsecondary school in the United States. It was originally called simply the New College, but it was renamed Harvard College on March 13, 1639, after John Harvard, the first principal donor to the new establishment.

By 1780, the new constitution of Massachusetts referred to Harvard as a "university."

Originally founded as a college to train new ministers, Harvard now has an endowment of over 22 billion dollars and is one of the most prestigious universities in the United States (as well as the world). It was the first of the eight famous "Ivy League" schools to be founded (see entry for October 14, 1937). Harvard is especially well known for its Business School, Kennedy School of Government, Law School, Medical School, and School of Education.

February 8, 1693— The College of William and Mary was chartered by King William III and Queen Mary II. The college was the second founded in the colonies behind Harvard University (see entry for September 8, 1636). William and Mary is located at Williamsburg, Virginia, and the college gained its initial fame from serving as the institution at which Thomas Jefferson was educated, starting in 1760.

William and Mary has a long-standing high academic reputation. Phi Beta Kappa, the nation's premier academic honor society, was formed at the college in 1776. William and Mary is one of only eight schools in the nation to be designated a "Public Ivy." This designation identifies state-assisted schools offering an education on a par with that of the Ivy League schools at a much lower cost. William and Mary became coeducational in 1918.

October 9, 1701— Yale University was founded by an "Act for Liberty to Erect a Collegiate School" passed by the General Court of the Colony of Connecticut. A group of 10 Congregationalist ministers met in Bramford, Connecticut, to pool their books for the school's first library. These ministers are known collectively as the Founders. The school opened in the home of its first rector, Abraham Pierson, in Killingworth, Connecticut. In 1716 the school moved to New Haven, Connecticut, where it still remains.

The school was originally known as the Collegiate School after the wording in the act that established it. Elihu Yale, a rich merchant at the time, was persuaded by Cotton Mather and others to help the fledging school. Yale donated nine bales of goods to the school, and their sale netted a substantial sum of money. The new school was thus renamed after its benefactor, and it has become world famous under the name of Yale University, one of the eight Ivy League schools (see entry for October 14, 1937). Harvard and Yale have been competitive both academically and athletically over the years in a way similar to Oxford and Cambridge in England.

Yale is especially well known for its Law School, School of Art, School of Drama, School of Medicine, and School of Music.

1746— The College of New Jersey was founded during this year. It later became known as Princeton University, one of the eight prestigious Ivy League schools (see entry for Ivy League on October 14, 1937). The university is located in the town of Princeton, New Jersey, situated geographically between Philadelphia and New York City. Princeton is especially notable for its Woodrow Wilson School of Public and International Affairs.

1751— The Academy of Philadelphia was founded in Philadelphia during this year. The school later became the University of Pennsylvania, the fourth in order of founding of the famous eight Ivy League universities (see entry for October 14, 1937). The university is notable for its Law School, School of Education, School of Medicine, School of Nursing, and Wharton School of Business.

1754— King's College was founded in New York City during this year. The college later became Columbia University, one of the eight prestigious Ivy League universities (see entry for October 14, 1937). Columbia is most known for its Business School, College of Physicians and Surgeons, Law School, School of Journalism, and Teacher's College.

1764— Rhode Island College was founded in Providence, Rhode Island, during this year. The college later became Brown University, one of the eight prestigious Ivy League universities (see entry for October 14, 1937). Although a diploma from Brown in any discipline it offers ranks highly, Brown is best known for its Medical School.

1769— Dartmouth College was founded in Hanover, New Hampshire, during this year. The school had earlier been founded in Connecticut in 1754, but was moved to New Hampshire and renamed Dartmouth College. It later became one of the eight prestigious Ivy League universities (see entry for October 14, 1937). Dartmouth is now best known for its Tuck School of Business, Medical School, and Thayer School of Engineering.

Dartmouth became known in a different way in the early 1800s as a result of the "Dartmouth College Issue" court ruling in 1818 (see listing). In a dispute between the son of the founder and the college trustees, the United States Supreme Court finally ruled that a private college could not be taken over by a state without the agreement of the private college. This was an important precedent for the founders of private colleges.

Dartmouth was the last of the Ivy League universities to be founded before the Revolutionary War. Except for Cornell, which was chartered in 1865 and opened October 7, 1868 (see listing), the Ivy League schools were all founded during colonial times. Harvard was founded first in 1636, and the next six schools were founded in 1701 (Yale), 1746 (Princeton), 1751 (University of Pennsylvania), 1754 (Columbia), 1764 (Brown), and 1769 (Dartmouth). (See preceding entries for each year.)

1783— During this year Noah Webster produced his own textbook for American children to use in school. Webster was a teacher who disliked the fact that American children had to use books imported from England in their early years in school. Webster's book was titled *A Grammatical Institute of the English Language*. It became known as the "Blue-backed Speller" because of its blue cover. For the next 100 years it taught children how to read, spell, and pronounce words.

Webster had been educated at Yale, which at the time was the only college in Connecticut (where Webster was born in 1758). After getting married in 1789 (he and his wife had eight children eventually), Webster moved for a while to Amherst, Massachusetts, where he helped start Amherst College. Returning to New Haven, Connecticut, where Yale was located, Webster started in 1801 at the age of 43 on the dictionary for which he would become world-famous. The effort consumed 27 years until Webster was 70 (see entry for April 14, 1828).

1785— The University of Georgia was chartered as the first state university in the United States, although it did not open until 1800. Other states (such as North Carolina, Vermont, and South Carolina) soon began to open state universities where no basic institute of higher education existed. Blount College opened in 1794 and later became the University of Tennessee.

1802— During this year Congress established the national military academy at West Point in New York State for the education and training of military officers. West Point had the first American training center for engineers.

1809— The first "public" or free school for the education of immigrants was opened during this year in New York City. It was built by the Free School Society, identified as Free School No. 1, and could seat 500 children in the enormous upper room of its two-floor structure. By 1840, half the population of New York City was foreign born.

1817— The University of Michigan was founded by the Michigan territorial legislature as one of the first public universities (as opposed to a private university) in the United States. It was built on land ceded by the Chippewa, Ottawa, and Potawatomi people "for a college at Detroit." The school moved to Ann Arbor, about 30 miles west of Detroit, in 1837. It has become a highly rated school, and for many years the most elite universities in the country were the Ivy League schools in the Northeast, Michigan in the middle of the country, and Stanford on the West Coast. These schools remain very highly rated, but other schools in other parts of the country have moved up to their level.

1817— Thomas Hopkins Gallaudet started his service as principal of what became The American School for the Deaf. This school was the first permanent school for deaf children established in the United States. Gallaudet was a minister who had graduated from Yale and the Andover Theological Seminary. He had toured Europe to find methods for educating deaf children at the request of Doctor Mason Cogwell, a neighbor in Hartford, Connecticut, who had a deaf daughter. The school was the answer to the doctor's problem.

Gallaudet served as principal of the school until 1830, when he retired to write children's books and took up other ministerial pursuits. His son, Dr. Edward Miner G. Gallaudet, helped create the famous school for the deaf near Washington, D.C., that became Gallaudet University, named after Thomas Hopkins Gallaudet (see entry for 1864). The original American School for the Deaf is still operating in Hartford.

1818— In a case setting an important precedent, the Supreme Court of the United States ruled that Dartmouth College (see entry for 1769), a private college, could not be taken over by a state against its will. In a dispute between the son of the founder of the college, John Wheelock, and its board of trustees, the decision of the trustees to remove Whitlock was essentially overthrown by a political maneuver to have Dartmouth converted to a state university. The trustees (and students) rebelled, and eventually won their case at the Supreme Court.

1821— The first public high school in the United States opened in Boston, Massachusetts, during this year. The school was originally called the English Classic School, but was renamed the English High School in 1824. The high school was initially intended for boys who did not plan to go on to college. Portland, Maine, and Worcester, Massachusetts, also opened public high schools soon afterwards. In 1825 the High School Society of New York City opened the first public high schools outside of New England.

A private school called the Boston Latin Grammar School had been founded in 1635 to prepare privileged young men to attend the college that became Harvard University (see listing for September 8, 1636), but there were no public (free) high schools in the United States until 1821.

March 1825— After many years of design, building, and assembling of a faculty, Thomas Jefferson was able to see his "ideal" institution, the University of Virginia, accept its first student body of 123 students during this month. They were all males, as Jefferson was a leading proponent of education, but not for females. The University of Virginia did not become truly coeducational until 1970 under the pressure of pending federal court suits. The school had agreed in 1920 to admit women over 20 years of age to some programs.

Located in Charlottesville, the university has long had a reputation as one of the leading academic schools in the nation. Jefferson would be proud of the university he founded, even though as a man of his times Jefferson did not intend it to offer educational opportunities to women and blacks. The university was integrated in the 1950s.

1827— During this year, the Commonwealth of Massachusetts passed a law requiring every town or village of 500 or more families (corresponding to a population of about 4,000) to open a high school. For about 50 years, Massachusetts was the only state that required high schools, but even there the law was largely ignored. As late as 1850, only about 60 percent of the towns large enough to require a high school actually had established one. Still, for many years, Massachusetts was considered the leading state in the nation in terms of education.

April 14, 1828— A copyright on Noah Webster's *American Dictionary of the English Language* was established. Webster had previously written a textbook teaching children how to read, spell, and pronounce words (see entry for 1783). He also had published a dictionary of the English language in 1806, but his ambition was to create a dictionary using the American version of the English language ("color" instead of "colour," and "music" instead of "musick," for example) and to include words that were used only in America ("skunk" and "squash," for example).

Webster felt Americans needed a standardized dictionary because words were spelled, pronounced, and used differently in different parts of the country. He tried to make the American spelling of words more phonetic, and he believed Americans should not necessarily speak and spell just like their ancestors in England. It took Webster 27 years, until the age of 70, to create a dictionary of this type with 70,000 entries.

Webster's dictionary was so popular that "Webster's" became synonymous with "dictionary." As a result, the "Webster's" name lost copyright protection and is now used by many publishers in the titles of their dictionaries. The Merriam brothers purchased the rights to revise Webster's dictionary from his heirs, and the *Merriam-Webster Dictionary* is considered the most direct descendant of Webster's lexicographical tradition. The 1913 version of this dictionary was very highly rated by scholars.

1829— During this year Dr. John Fisher applied for and received a charter from the Commonwealth of Massachusetts to establish a school to educate the blind. A trip to Paris by Fisher in the early 1820s, when he was a medical student, brought him in contact with the world's first school for the blind, and he determined to establish such a school in the United States. Samuel Gridely Howe, the director of the school, started teaching a few students in 1832 using rooms in his father's Boston home. This small beginning became the world-famous Perkins School for the Blind.

In 1833 the school moved into a larger home owned by Thomas Perkins, who was a trustee and vice president of the school. By 1839 there were 65 students, and Perkins sold his home and donated the proceeds to the school so it could take over and convert a hotel in South Boston. The school was renamed after Perkins as a result.

In the meantime, in 1837, Laura Bridgman enrolled in the school and eventually became the first documented deaf-blind person to be educated. Helen Keller would be educated as well at the Perkins School in 1888 (see entry for March 3, 1887).

December, 1833— Oberlin College was opened during this month. It was founded by Presbyterian minister John L. Shiperd, and was named after the town of Oberlin, Ohio, in which it was located. Oberlin became the first truly coeducational college in the United States in 1837, and in 1841 three of its women graduates became the first in the nation to receive bachelor's degrees.

Controversy swirled around Oberlin practically from the time it opened. In 1835, the trustees of Lane Theological Seminary prohibited its students from discussing slavery, hoping to avoid conflicts over this emotional issue. Instead, conflicts arose over the issue of free speech, and one trustee, one professor, and several students left Lane and ended up at Oberlin. The trustee, Asa Mahan, was offered the presidency of Oberlin. He accepted on the conditions that Oberlin permit free speech and also admit black students.

Oberlin had intended to also admit both men and women when it first opened, and its first student body of 44 students included 15 women. These women, however, were only admitted to the College Preparatory program. By 1837, women were admitted on the same basis as men, making Oberlin the first truly coeducational college in the United Sates. Oberlin further became one of the first colleges to admit blacks, and its students were active participants in the Underground Railroad that helped escaped slaves obtain their freedom.

Possibly because of its unique student body mix in its early controversial days, Oberlin has achieved an impressive reputation for its music programs. It presently enrolls about 500 students in its Conservatory of Music division to go along with about 2,600 students enrolled in its College of Arts and Sciences.

1836— The first of the famous *McGuffey Readers* was published during this year. These books were intended to permit children to learn to read and advance through progressively more difficult levels by moving on to the next reader in the series. They were intended to take the reader through the sixth grade. For about three-quarters of a century the readers were used by about 80 percent of all American schoolchildren. Over 122 million copies of the readers were sold, and with an estimated five to seven children sharing each book, their influence was enormous. Even today over 100,000 copies are printed, mostly for home schooling use.

At the beginning of the process, the publishing company of Truman and Smith had invited William Holmes McGuffey to write a series of reading textbooks aimed at the western market. McGuffey was an ordained Presbyterian minister who was a professor of ancient languages at Miami University in Ohio. He had earlier experience as a schoolmaster, and is thought to have published in London a book about methods of reading. McGuffey signed a contract in 1833 that gave him royalties of 10 percent up to a maximum of $1,000, a good sum at the time. After that, the publisher kept all the profit. It was eventually a bonanza for the publisher.

McGuffey, with the aid of sample textbooks sent by the publishers, completed the *First* and *Second Readers* in time for publication in 1836. They were originally called the Eclectic Series without any mention of the author's name. The *Third* and *Fourth Readers* appeared the following year. This initial series started out with a *Primer*, *Pictorial Primer*, *Progressive Speller*, and then the *First* through *Fourth Readers*. The stories were about the values of various virtues and the rewards of old-fashioned hard work, patriotism, reverence for God, and respect for parents. There were finally a Fifth and Sixth Reader published several years later.

The involvement of McGuffey in the series ended in about 1843. Supposedly his wife actually wrote the *Primer*, and his younger brother wrote the later *Fifth* and *Sixth Readers*. Then a number of writers were involved in making constant revisions to the readers that were very helpful in maintaining their popularity until 1900 or so, when the United States was a far less rural nation than it had been in 1836. The *Readers* were especially popular in the West and the Mississippi River valley, but they were read in all states of the union. They introduced many readers to excerpts from the classics, including Shakespeare, while they also established the popularity of such poems as "Mary had a Little Lamb" and "Twinkle, Twinkle Little Star."

1837— During this year, a Philadelphia Quaker made a bequest to ensure that blacks had access to education, and the Institute of Colored Youth was born. It moved from Philadelphia to the nearby suburb of Cheyney in 1903. The school ultimately became Cheyney University after being purchased by the Commonwealth of Pennsylvania and joining the collection of teacher's colleges established in the state.

Cheyney was the first of what is called Historically Black Colleges and Universities (HBCU). Being established before the Morrill Land-Grant Act (1862) and the end of the Civil War (1865) made the school indeed historical, even if it started out as a school offering only an elementary and high school education.

November 8, 1837— Mount Holyoke Female Seminary in Massachusetts opened its doors. It was the first institution of higher education in the United States intended only for women. Mount Holyoke obtained collegiate status in 1888 and became Mount Holyoke Seminary and College. In 1893 the seminary curriculum was dropped and the school became simply Mount Holyoke College.

Based on its original founding date of 1837, Mount Holyoke was the first of the so-called Seven Sisters, seven prestigious colleges located in the Northeastern United States originally intended only for women. They were Barnard, Bryn Mawr, Mount Holyoke, Radcliffe, Smith, Vassar, and Wellesley (see individual listing for each school in the index, and the Seven Sisters listing in 1927). For over 125 years after Mount Holyoke opened, attending one of these seven schools was a prime goal for women seeking a college education.

Mary Lyon was the key force behind Mount Holyoke, traveling tirelessly in the early 1800s for almost two decades to raise funds to create her vision of a college for women. Once it was established, the school was noted for developing teachers, and for specifying that the curriculum should emphasize academic subjects and specifically should not contain domestic pursuits.

1839— The first state-sponsored "normal" school (a school for the specific training of teachers) was opened in Lexington, Massachusetts.

1846— The New York City Public (Free) School Society was replaced by the New York City Board of Education. The board members were publicly elected. The Public School Society was felt by many immigrants to be an elite group with a distinctly Protestant bias in its teachings and in the school-books used in its schools.

1850—What became the National Education Association (NEA) was founded this year by Robert Campbell under the name National Teachers Association. The present name was adopted in 1857. The NEA is the largest union of teachers in the United States. It includes teachers at all levels from nursery school to universities, totaling 2.7 million members. With an operating budget of $150 million, it is a very powerful organization. The NEA is not a member of the AFL-CIO as is its smaller rival, the American Federation of Teachers (AFT). The NEA and AFT did not go through with an NEA-proposed merger in 1998. Instead, the two organizations nominally cooperate through the "NEAFT Partnership."

1850—An activist Catholic priest named John Hughes was made archbishop of New York. He used his considerable powers to help create a privately funded national system of Catholic schools. This system grew to become the largest alternative school system in the United States.

1854—Lincoln University, a college intended to provide higher education for blacks, was founded during this year under the name of Ashmun Institute. In 1866 the school, located just north of the Mason-Dixon Line in southeastern Pennsylvania not far from Philadelphia, was renamed in honor of President Lincoln. An important college for blacks since its inception, Lincoln University graduated about 20 percent of all black physicians and 10 percent of all black lawyers in the United States during the first 100 years of its existence.

In spite of being a beacon of service for a minority race, it was not until 1952 that women were permitted to attend the university.

1855—A law was passed by the legislature of Massachusetts abolishing segregation in the public schools of the state. The passage of this law was the end result of a series of court battles pursued by Benjamin Roberts, a black man who tried to enroll his daughter in better schools in Boston that were also closer to her home. Blacks were permitted to go to school in the North during this pre–Civil War era, but they were not permitted to go to schools with whites. The Massachusetts state supreme court had turned down Roberts in 1849 on essentially the "separate but equal" concept. This concept held sway in the United States until almost 100 years later when the *Brown v. Board of Education* ruling was made in 1954 (see entry).

After being denied by the state supreme court, Roberts took his case to the state legislature, which eventually responded with the nonsegregation law in 1855. It was the first such law in the United States.

1856— During this year, Magarethe Meyer Schurz opened the first kindergarten in the United States in Watertown, Wisconsin. Mrs. Schurz, who had studied under Friedrich Frobel, the developer of the kindergarten idea in Germany, employed his techniques to instruct her daughter Agathe, and four neighborhood children.

Frobel designed the kindergarten in Germany in 1837 to provide an educational environment less formal than an elementary school, but one that would organize children's play instincts in a constructive way. This would help children prepare for their first years in elementary school. The word "kindergarten" in German means literally a "garden of children."

Mrs. Schurz attracted the attention of other neighbors, and even though her school was taught in her native German language (as were most early kindergartens in the United States), the school flourished until World War I. Then it was closed because of opposition to the use of the German language.

1856— During this year Wilberforce University was founded in Wilberforce, Ohio. It was the first black college founded for women, and was the oldest black liberal arts college founded in the United States. The college was named after the eighteenth century English statesman and abolitionist William Wilberforce. It is associated with the African Methodist Episcopal Church, and it was the first institution of higher education for blacks to be owned and operated by blacks. Cheyney and Lincoln University (see listings) predated Wilberforce, but they were not owned by blacks.

December 1856— Henry Barnard, a noted school reformer, published an article in the *American Journal of Education* titled "Gradation of Public Schools with Special Reference to Cities and Large Villages." The article was about the then-new practice of dividing public schools into "grades." In this approach, the same teacher would teach everyone in a specific grade the same subjects for one year, and the students would move to a new grade at the end of the year depending on their performance in the previous grade.

This method lent itself to teaching certain subjects in specific blocks of time, and it was easily adjusted to fit new students flowing in ever greater numbers into the schools. The days of the old one-room schoolhouse were numbered. By 1860 the graded school was common in large cities, and by 1870, the practice was common almost everywhere there were enough students to divide into the graded approach. The practice is, of course, still with us.

1859— The Cooper Union for the Advancement of Science and Art was founded during this year in New York City. The Cooper Union was a high-light in educational history when it opened, and even today it is the "only full-scholarship college in the United States dedicated exclusively to prepar-ing students for the professions of architecture, art, and engineering."

Peter Cooper was the son of an uneducated workingman, and Peter himself had less than one year of formal education. Yet Peter Cooper became an industrialist and inventor. He designed and built the first railroad steam engine in the United States. He made a fortune running a glue factory and an iron foundry, and went on to successful ventures in real estate, insurance, railroads, and telegraphy. He even ran once for president. To top off his varied career, he invented instant gelatin, to which his wife added fruit. The concoction became known as Jell-O.

Cooper's lack of education always bothered him, and even as one of the richest men in the nation, he could not spell. He determined to build a school to offer a free college education to the children (both boys and girls) of the working class, of which he was once a member. He had the Cooper Union built, and it was one of the first colleges to offer a free education to working-class children and also to women. Cooper's example was credited with inspiring Andrew Carnegie, Ezra Cornell, and Matthew Vassar to use their fortunes to build colleges as well.

Cooper Union also provided a public library and free public reading room (the first in New York City), as well as an auditorium offering free sci-entific lectures and a rostrum for public speakers such as Abraham Lincoln when he was running for president. In many ways The Cooper Union (orig-inally commonly known as the Cooper Institute) was the prototype for what we now know as "continuing education."

1860— In this year Elizabeth Peabody started a private English-speaking kindergarten in Boston after Peabody had visited the German-speaking kindergarten started in Wisconsin by Mrs. Carl Schurz (see entry for 1856). Peabody became a vocal advocate of the kindergarten idea as an indispens-able part of education in the United States. The idea spread widely in the East due to Peabody's efforts. It also spread quickly in the upper Midwest, where many German immigrants had settled and were already familiar with the concept. It became part of the public school system in the United States, a practice prompted by the opening of the first public school kindergarten in St. Louis by Susan Blow in 1873 (see entry for 1873).

April 10, 1861— The Commonwealth of Massachusetts offered a charter to the Massachusetts Institute of Technology. The college (known by its ini-tials as MIT) was founded by distinguished natural scientist William B.

Rogers, who wanted to create a new kind of educational institution that would be relevant to an increasingly industrialized nation. The Civil War delayed the opening of the college, and it did not admit its first students until 1865.

MIT quickly established a high reputation for its science and engineering courses, but by 1900 the college was having financial difficulties. A merger was proposed with nearby Harvard University, which had plenty of cash but was much weaker in the sciences than in liberal arts. However, an outcry by the alumni of MIT caused the merger to be cancelled. In 1916 MIT moved across the river from Harvard to it present location in Cambridge, Massachusetts.

World War II brought great prominence to MIT as its soon-to-be-famous "Radiation Laboratories" played the major role in the development of radar, which many scientists claimed played a bigger part in winning the war than the more dramatic atomic bomb. The "Rad Lab" series of books published after the war became required reading for engineers across the nation. When *Sputnik* was launched by Soviet Russia in 1957, it firmly cemented the relationship between the United States military and MIT in terms of research funds being poured into the college to develop high-technology defense projects. MIT is also well known for its contributions to the development of the personal computer and the Internet.

MIT is essentially now a national resource in the sciences and engineering, and is one of the most difficult colleges in the country to enter, accepting only 16 percent of those who apply. It is a coeducational institution with over 4,000 undergraduates, consisting of 57 percent men and 43 percent women.

MIT established another kind of history in 2001 when its president admitted that the institution had severely restricted the careers of women faculty members and researchers in the past, and it now was taking steps to redress the issue. In August 2004, Susan Hockfield, a molecular neurobiologist, was appointed MIT's first female president.

July 2, 1862 — President Abraham Lincoln signed the Morrill Land-Grant Act into law. This act was one of the most important pieces of legislation ever created in terms of establishing colleges and universities in the United States. Justin Smith Morrill was a representative and later a senator from Vermont. He introduced his first land-grant bill in 1857, and after a struggle in getting it through Congress he was disappointed to see it vetoed by President Buchanan. Morrill tried again in 1862, when the absence due to the Civil War of southern legislators, who had opposed the earlier bill and had encouraged its veto, made it easier to pass the bill the second time around.

The Morrill Act contained many elements that Jonathan Turner, a graduate of Yale and a farmer, editor, and college professor, had proposed earlier in an effort to create state universities for the "Industrial Classes," including farmers. The Morrill Act stated that the land-grant colleges would include classes in agriculture, engineering, and home economics as well as traditional subjects. The act also established provisions for military training, now known as the Reserve Officer Training Corps (ROTC). This was a popular element of the act at the time of the Civil War.

The act gave 30,000 acres of land to the states for each representative and senator the state had. These lands were to be used to build and support public universities (as opposed to the Ivy League schools, for example, that were private institutions). The federal government also supplied funds to assist in the operation of the schools, and the Department of Agriculture helped greatly in establishing and supporting the agriculture experimental stations that were the hallmark of the original schools.

The land-grant schools essentially opened the doors of college to the nonelite of the country. They also offered educations in subjects well beyond the somewhat narrow "classical" curricula of many of the existing colleges of the time. There are now 105 land-grant institutions in the United States, including at least one in every state and territory, and they receive about $550 million annually in federal support. Many subsequent amendments and related legislative items have been added to the original Morrill Act to expand the land-grant college concept.

1864— The school that became Gallaudet University, the only university in the world in which all programs and services are designed to accommodate deaf students, was essentially founded during this year when President Abraham Lincoln signed a bill permitting the Columbia Institution for the Instruction of the Deaf and Dumb and the Blind, created in 1857, to confer college degrees. The school was soon named the Columbia Institution for the Deaf and Dumb (the blind students were transferred to another school), and the college division became the National Deaf-Mute College.

Dr. Edward Miner Gallaudet, son of Thomas Hopkins Gallaudet, founder of the first school for the deaf in the United States (see entry for 1817), was president of the new operation. Later, in 1893, the name of the college was changed to Gallaudet College in honor of the elder Gallaudet. The college grew over the decades to become famous around the world for developing programs and techniques for the education of deaf people of all ages.

March 3, 1865— The Bureau of Refugees, Freedmen, and Abandoned Lands was established by an act of Congress. It became known as the Freedmen's Bureau, and it was a prime mover in setting up black schools to help blacks become self-sufficient. However, these schools were kept segregated by a series of "Black Codes" that quickly arose in southern states in response to the establishment of the Freedmen's Bureau.

September 26, 1865—Vassar Female College opened in Poughkeepsie, New York, with 353 students enrolled. The college was financed by wealthy Matthew Vassar. It was chartered by the New York Legislature in January 1861, three months before Fort Sumter was fired upon and the Civil War began. Building went on during the war, and the college was finally ready for occupancy in September 1865. Eighteen months later the word "female" was dropped from the title of the college, although it remained a college for women only.

Vassar became one of the famous Seven Sisters, the group of prestigious colleges for women located in the northeastern United States (see Seven Sisters listing in 1927). Vassar was the first of the Sisters to become a coeducational school, welcoming its first male undergraduates in 1969. At the time, it was felt that this would eliminate a kind of "reverse discrimination" against men that was no longer suitable in the liberated 1960s. Ironically, the first Vassar male graduate to run for political office was Rick Lazio, class of 1989, who, although successfully elected to Congress, was later defeated in a Senate race by a graduate of Wellesley College, another of the Seven Sisters.

November 20, 1865—Two former slaves, William Savery and Thomas Tarrant, who lived in Talladega, Alabama, met in a convention of new freedmen in Mobile, Alabama, and decided to form a school for the children of former slaves. This was the beginning of Talladega College.

The two former slaves were assisted by General Wagner Swayne of the Freedmen's Bureau (see listing for March 3, 1865), and these leaders built a one-room school using lumber salvaged from an abandoned carpenter's shop. Soon the need for new quarters was evident, and the school focused on a nearby Baptist academy that was about to be sold due to a mortgage default. The academy had originally been built by slaves, including Savery and Tarrant, and General Swayne was able to arrange the purchase of the building and surrounding land by the American Missionary Association. The resulting school, opened in 1867 to 140 students, was named the Swayne School. It was the first school opened in Alabama for blacks, and its origin was a school built for white students by black slaves.

In 1869, Swayne School was issued a charter as Talladega College by the Judge of Probate of Talladega County.

December 1, 1865—Henry Martin Tupper started a theology class as a means of teaching black freedmen to read and interpret the Bible. This humble beginning was the start of Shaw University in Raleigh, North Carolina, the oldest black college in the South. Rapid growth in the size of the class led to the purchase of land in 1866 for the purpose of erecting a building to serve as both a church and school. The school was named the Raleigh Institute, but the name was changed to the Shaw Collegiate Institute in 1870 in honor of Elijah Shaw, a benefactor who provided funds for the first new building. In 1875, the school was incorporated as Shaw University and was declared open to students without regard to race, creed, or sex.

January 9, 1866— On this date Fisk University convened its first classes of former slaves in facilities in former Union Army barracks in Nashville, Tennessee. The school was named in honor of General Clinton B. Fisk of the Tennessee Freedmen's Bureau, who arranged the facilities for the school.

November 1866— During this month 10 members of the First Congregation Society of Washington, D.C., met to develop plans for a theological seminary for the training of black ministers. This school was initially named the Howard Normal and Theological Institute for the Education of Teachers and Preachers, but by January 8, 1867, it was named Howard University. The school was granted a charter by Congress on March 2, 1867. The name was in honor of General Oliver T. Howard, a Civil War hero, who was commissioner of the Freedmen's Bureau (see listing), and who was one of the founders of the school.

Howard University, the third university to be founded in Washington, D.C., behind Georgetown and George Washington universities, became a leading law school for blacks in the following years. Two of its graduates were Charles Hamilton Houston and Thurgood Marshall, who played the leading roles in directing the National Association for the Advancement of Colored People (NAACP — see listing) to victory in the legal battles that ended segregation in public schools in 1954.

March 23, 1868— A merger of two existing schools formed the University of California, which grew with the State College System (see 1960 entry) to be the largest combined university system in the United States (and in the world), as California grew to be the most populous state in the United States.

A private school called the College of California had been founded in Oakland by a Congregational minister named Henry Durant in 1855. In response to the Morrill Act (see entry for 1862), a state school called the Agricultural, Mining, and Mechanical Arts College was established in 1866. The College of California had recently purchased a tract of land for expansion four miles north of their Oakland holdings in a place they named Berkeley, but the college had limited operating funds. The new land grant college had ample public funds, but no suitable land. A merger on March 23, 1868, solved the problems of both schools. The resulting University of California started in Oakland, but moved to Berkeley in 1873. It is still located there in a much-expanded fashion.

The University of California gained much national recognition during World War II, when Ernest O. Lawrence and Glenn T. Seaborg made major contributions to the development of the atomic bomb. J. Robert Oppenheimer, who directed the building of the bomb at Los Alamos, New Mexico, was a physics professor at the University of California. The university took on the task of managing the bomb project, and also of managing the Lawrence Livermore National Laboratory and the Los Alamos National Laboratory. Major observatories (the Lick Observatory and the Keck Observatory) are also managed by the University of California.

In 1952 a major restructuring of the University of California system resulted in a separate entity being established at the Berkeley campus with separate chancellors being established for the Berkeley campus (and other campuses) as well as the overall university system. Ultimately a University of California president was appointed by the state-appointed regents to head the overall system. The University of California system has continued to grow ever since. The overall University of California System (not to be confused with the even larger California State University System — see 1960 entry) now has 191,000 students spread out over 10 campuses in the state. A faculty of 13,335 serves these students.

April 1, 1868— The Hampton Normal and Agricultural Institute, soon generally known as Hampton Institute, opened its doors. The purpose of the institute was to provide an education for freed slaves. Land and financial support were provided by the American Missionary Association of New York, but the institute was essentially founded by General Samuel Chapman Armstrong, who was also its first principal.

Armstrong was the son of Hawaiian educational missionaries, and he was studying in Virginia when he was called to lead the Ninth United States Colored Troops Regiment in the Union Army during the Civil War. After the war, Armstrong was assigned to the so-called Freedman's Bureau that was designed to help the newly freed slaves. Armstrong found this effort to be not nearly enough, in his opinion, and with the financial help of the missionary society, he founded a vocational school to help educate the ex-slaves.

The Hampton Institute, located in Hampton, Virginia, near Washington, D.C., was basically a vocational school. Mornings were spent in religious and academic activities, and afternoons were spent learning blacksmithing, carpentry, cooking, dressmaking, farming, laundering, sewing, and shoemaking.

Hampton agreed in 1878 to admit Native Americans who had been held as prisoners of war after the Civil War. The success of Hampton in this effort led to the founding of the Indian school near Carlisle, Pennsylvania, that later produced the famous Jim Thorp. In addition, Hampton served as a model for Booker T. Washington when Washington formed Tuskegee Institute in 1881 to provide education for blacks. Thus, Armstrong's work to provide a much-needed educational opportunity for the freed slaves had positive repercussions well beyond the environs of Hampton Institute.

July 28, 1868 — The Fourteenth Amendment to the Constitution was ratified after being proposed on June 13, 1866. Twenty-eight of the 37 states ratified the amendment by July 1868. The other nine states eventually ratified it (some as late as 1976). Southern states were required to ratify it in order to be readmitted to the Union, and most refused. However, official ratification by the other states made the issue moot. Southern states then used the so-called "Slaughterhouse Cases" of 1873 to get the courts to narrowly define federal power. This largely emasculated the amendment by asserting that most of the rights of citizens remained under state control.

The amendment overruled the infamous Dred Scott decision of 1857 that ruled blacks could not be citizens. The Fourteenth Amendment guaranteed that all persons born or naturalized in the United States are citizens of the United States and of the state in which they reside, and that no state shall abridge the privileges and immunities of citizens, shall deprive any person of life, liberty, or property without due process of law, or shall deny to any person the equal protection of the law.

This amendment would become the basis for the eventual end of segregation, although, as noted, many states issued laws that would make segregation an issue of state's rights after the amendment was ratified. It would take more than another three-quarters of a century before segregation in public schools was declared unconstitutional in 1954.

October 7, 1868 — Opening-day ceremonies were held in Ithaca, New York, for 412 students of Cornell University. The school had been chartered in 1865 by Ezra Cornell (who donated the funds and the land to get the school started), and state senator Andrew Dickson White, who became Cornell's first president and helped it become a land-grant institution. Cornell later became one of the eight prestigious Ivy League universities (see entry for October 14, 1937). Cornell was the last of the Ivy League schools to be founded, as the previous seven schools had been founded in 1769 or before (the first school, Harvard, had been founded in 1636). But Cornell was unique among the Ivy League schools in that it was founded as a coeducational university from the start. The remainder of the Ivy League universities would not become fully coeducational until the 1980s.

Cornell is best known now for its College of Engineering, Law School, Weill Medical School, and the School of Hotel Administration, and in conjunction with the state university of New York, for the NYS College of Agriculture and Life Sciences and the NYS College of Veterinary Medicine.

March 17, 1870— Wellesley College of Massachusetts was chartered. The college was founded by Henry Fowle Durant and Pauline Fowle Durant to "provide an excellent liberal arts education for women who will make a difference in the world." The college became one of the Seven Sisters, a group of prestigious colleges for women in the northeastern United States (see entry for Seven Sisters in 1927).

1873— During this year Susan Blow founded the first public school kindergarten in the United States, in St. Louis, Missouri. Before this time kindergartens were either private or parochial (see kindergarten entries for 1856 and 1860). She was assisted in her work by William T. Harris, superintendent of schools in St. Louis. Later, Blow would write and Harris would edit a book called *Letters to a Mother on the Philosophy of Frobel.* Friederich Frobel was the founder of the kindergarten system in Germany in 1837.

The St. Louis model was emulated over the entire United States in the following years. By the 1920s kindergartens were generally part of public school systems in all parts of the United States.

1874— An important ruling by the Michigan Supreme Court during this year greatly helped the growth of high schools everywhere in the United States. Many people at the time felt high schools were not really an important part of the educational process. Such people felt high schools primarily prepared elite children to apply for college, and thus these groups felt they should not be taxed to pay for high schools. A group of taxpayers brought suit in Kalamazoo, Michigan, to prevent the town from collecting and utilizing taxes to support the new high school there.

The case reached the Michigan Supreme Court, and in 1874 the court ruled that high schools are indeed "common schools" (the term used then to identify free public schools that children started around age six), and that high schools represented a vital link between elementary schools and the state university. The absence of public (free) secondary schools would discriminate in favor of the rich, who could afford tuition-based high schools. This discrimination would prevent anyone other than rich people from entering college.

Although other such cases came to trial, the Kalamazoo decision became a precedent that established the right of several states to levy taxes for public high schools. This precedent contributed to the great growth of high schools in the period before World War I.

1875— Smith College, chartered in 1871, was opened this year in Northampton, Massachusetts, following the terms of the will of Sophia Smith, who died in 1870 as the last remaining member of the wealthy Smith family. The plan for the women's college may have owed as much to Smith's advisor, the Reverend John Greene, as to Sophia Smith, and Greene was among the first trustees of the college.

Smith College grew to be one of the largest and most respected colleges for women in the United States, and it was counted as one of the Seven Sisters, the group of prestigious women's colleges located in the northeastern United States (see entry for Seven Sisters in 1927).

February 22, 1876— Johns Hopkins University officially opened its doors simultaneously with the inauguration of its first president, Daniel Colt Gilman. Johns Hopkins, the wealthy businessman after whom the university was named, had incorporated both a hospital and a university in 1867. Hopkins died in 1873 at the age of 78, but before his death he directed that the hospital must provide surgical or medical services for the poor of the city and its environs regardless of sex, age, or color. He also directed that the hospital have a school of medicine and a school of nursing.

In October 1874, the trustees of the university incorporated by Hopkins asked Daniel Colt Gilman, then president of the University of California in Berkeley to consider becoming president of Johns Hopkins University and to build a new university from scratch. Gilman accepted the offer, and after a year of preliminary work, was officially inaugurated in 1876, as noted above.

Gilman proceeded to build a research university, an idea then new to the United States, which advanced not only the knowledge of students, but also advanced the state of human knowledge generally through research and scholarship. This idea was revolutionary at the time, but it led to the research university system in the United States as it exists today. The School of Medicine at Johns Hopkins, associated with the Johns Hopkins Hospital, is now one of the most famous in the world.

In recent years, Johns Hopkins has received more federal research and development funding than any other university. This is due in large measure to its applied physics laboratory. But its School of Medicine is the largest recipient of grants from the National Institutes of Health, and the university's Bloomberg School of Public Health, the first of its kind in the United States, ranks first among public health schools in federal research support. The university has succeeded very well in its mission as a research university, but it also presently offers courses in nearly every discipline of education.

1879—A group of men and women led by Elizabeth Cary Agassiz created the "Harvard Annex" for women's instruction by the Harvard faculty during this year. Fifteen years later, in 1894, the Annex was chartered as Radcliffe College by the Commonwealth of Massachusetts. Radcliffe became one of the famous Seven Sisters, a group of prestigious women's colleges in the northeastern United States (see entry for Seven Sisters in 1927).

Although well established as a highly desirable women's college, Radcliffe continued over the years to try to permit women to become undergraduates at Harvard on an equal basis with men. In 1943, during World War II, Harvard and Radcliffe signed an agreement to allow women students into Harvard classrooms for the first time. In 1963, Harvard's Graduate School of Arts was opened to women, and Radcliffe's graduate school was closed. In the 1970s the schools essentially merged, with women being granted Harvard degrees (the first joint Harvard and Radcliffe commencement was held in 1970). All limits on the number of women Harvard undergraduates was eliminated in 1975. The merger was formally finalized in 1999, and the Radcliffe Institute for Advanced Study was created as one of 10 Harvard schools. Radcliffe had been so successful in "integrating" the previously all-male Harvard that the need for Radcliffe as a stand-alone school was eliminated.

1880—During this year the Samuel P. Hayes Research Library was established at the Perkins School for the Blind in Boston (see entry for 1829). The library has grown to be the largest repository of its kind in the world. It contains the most recent and most complete information on the nonmedical aspects of blindness and deaf-blindness. It includes many books by and about Helen Keller, who was initially educated at Perkins (see entry for March 3, 1887).

June 27, 1880—A baby girl was born to Captain Arthur Keller and his wife, Kate Keller, in Tuscumbia, Alabama. She was named Helen, and less than two years later, in February of 1882, the girl was struck by a mysterious disease that left her deaf and blind. This was a great personal tragedy, but it was also the beginning of one of the most dramatic stories in the history of education. Helen Keller, although deaf and blind before she was two, would become a college graduate who would publish books and give lectures to audiences around the world (see entry for March 3, 1887).

July 4, 1881—Tuskegee Institute opened its doors. Tuskegee was founded by Booker T. Washington following the vocational model set by Hampton Institute, which had opened in 1868 (see listing). Washington had a somewhat different student body in that the black students in his first class already had some level of education. Washington was determined to develop them into teachers who would return to the plantation districts and show the blacks there "how to put new energy and new ideas into farming as well as into the intellectual, moral, and religious life of the people."

The State of Alabama had, in response to the urgings of both a former slave and former slave owner, agreed to provide $2,000 for teachers' salaries for such an institution, but nothing for land, buildings, or equipment. The first class of 30 students met in a dilapidated church and shanty. The students developed their craft and occupational skills by making and laying bricks and assembling buildings. They developed their agricultural skills by learning to farm and to feed themselves. They earned compensation to pay for future tuition. Washington stressed that industrial education would be the basis on which "habits of thrift, a love of work, ownership of property and bank accounts" would grow. Washington emphasized what he called "total education," insisting on personal cleanliness and high moral character.

Although other black leaders would later criticize Washington for being too accommodating to white restrictions, Washington knew that only so much was possible in the post–Reconstruction era in which bitter whites were developing a segregationist society. A famous quote by Washington expressed his views on how blacks should concentrate on becoming productive even if various parts of society were presently closed to them. He said that "the opportunity to earn a dollar in a factory just now is worth infinitely more than the opportunity to spend a dollar in an opera house."

With this attitude, Washington was able to gain widespread support in both the North and the South. The school moved in 1882 to 100 acres of abandoned farmland, purchased with a personal loan of $200 from the treasurer of Hampton Institute. Washington traveled extensively making speeches to gather support. Buildings were erected on the new campus bearing the names of their benefactors, including Andrew Carnegie, Collis P. Huntington, and John D. Rockefeller.

By the time Washington died in 1915, 34 years after he founded the institute, Tuskegee had become internationally famous. Today it has grown to over 160 buildings on a campus of nearly 270 acres encompassing 5,000 students and staff. After furnishing many blacks with a successful vocational education and supplying many black educators as well, Tuskegee now also offers a conventional college degree-granting program that began in 1927.

1885— Bryn Mawr College, named after the small Pennsylvania town near Philadelphia in which the college was located, was founded during this year. It was founded to give women educational opportunities long denied to them, including the first Ph.D. program at a women's college. Bryn Mawr became one of the Seven Sisters, a group of prestigious colleges for women in the northeastern United States (see entry for Seven Sisters in 1927).

November 11, 1885 — Leland Stanford, railroad magnate and governor of California, made a founding grant on this date to create what is now commonly known as Stanford University. The official title of the school is Leland Stanford Junior University, as it was named after the deceased teenage son of Leland Stanford and his wife Jane. However, it is normally referred to as simply Stanford University, or sometimes locally as "The Farm" in remembrance of its origin as a horse farm.

The cornerstone of the first building was laid on May 14, 1887, and the university officially opened on October 1, 1891. The first student body numbered 559 students, who enjoyed free tuition. Although Stanford was nominally founded as a coeducational school, female enrollment was capped for many years. Stanford has grown to enjoy as much prestige as the Ivy League schools, ranking as one of the best universities in the United States and the world, even though it was founded 250 years later than Harvard.

1887 — During this year, G. Stanley Hall founded the *American Journal of Psychology*. Hall was a psychologist associated with Johns Hopkins University during most of his career. He was especially interested in the education of adolescents, and he used his magazine to promote his ideas that high schools should be focused on the general education of their students rather than serving primarily as a college preparatory institution. He stressed the need for "child-centered" education, but also supported the use of various tests (including the so-called IQ test) to determine a child's mental abilities and intellectual strengths and weaknesses.

March 3, 1887 — Anne Sullivan arrived in Tuscumbia, Alabama, to serve as a teacher for the deaf and blind Helen Keller, now nearly seven years old. Sullivan was recommended by Michael Anagnos, director of the Perkins Institute for the Blind in Boston (see entry for 1829). Anagnos in turn had been recommended to the Kellers by Alexander Graham Bell, whom the Kellers had met with in the summer of 1886. Bell was famous for his invention of the telephone a decade earlier, but Bell had been known as a teacher of the hearing-impaired before he turned his attention to the telephone (which he initially pursued as a potentially improved way of teaching those with hearing defects).

Sullivan was a star pupil and valedictorian of her class of 1886 at the Perkins Institute. She was initially nearly blind due to an eye infection, but a series of operations had essentially restored her sight by the time she graduated at the age of 20. But at the Perkins school, Sullivan had learned the manual alphabet, or "manual sign language," and this is how she made her initial contact with Helen Keller.

Keller had had a previous affinity for water as a toddler before she contracted her mysterious disease, and by one month after Sullivan's arrival, Sullivan had taught Keller to connect the manual signal for water with the water that flowed over their hands from the family pump (in a scene made famous 70 years later in the play and movie *The Miracle Worker*). From this small beginning, Sullivan went on to teach Keller how to communicate with the world around her in spite of her serious handicaps. Sullivan became a lifelong companion of Keller, a situation the Kellers could, fortunately, afford to support.

October 17, 1887 — The first student body of 12 young adults began classes at the new Pratt Institute in New York City. Founded by oil entrepreneur Charles Pratt, the institute originally focused on training industrial workers for the emerging industrial economy of the United States. The Institute has always stressed the concept that the prime task of a college is to provide an education that will enable its students to meet the changing needs of the economy.

Charles Pratt was one of 11 children of a carpenter. He scraped together enough money to attend some courses at Wesleyan Academy in Massachusetts. He eventually gained control of a whale oil business in New York, which he later merged with Standard Oil, building his fortune. Because of his limited education, he wanted to open an institution where students could learn trades through the skillful use of their hands. Pratt Institute was the result, although Pratt died only four years after the school opened. But his sons kept the institute growing.

Pratt Institute presently offers a full range of courses, including architecture, art and design, information and library science, and liberal arts and sciences. It has the oldest continuous library science program in the United States. When it opened it marked another step in offering college courses to nonelite working-class students.

October 1889 — Barnard College welcomed its first class of 14 students, all of whom were women. The college was located in New York City, and in 1898 it moved to Morningside Heights, where Columbia University was located. Barnard became affiliated with Columbia in 1900, but Barnard remained governed by its own trustees, faculty, and dean. Barnard was also responsible for its own endowment and facilities. However, Barnard shared with Columbia the instructors, the library, and the degree of the university.

Barnard became one of the Seven Sisters, a group of prestigious women's colleges in the northeastern United States (see entry for Seven Sisters in

1927). But in 1983 Columbia began to accept women applicants on its own, ending Barnard's exclusive right to do so.

1891— Drexel Institute was founded in Philadelphia during this year. Financier Anthony J. Drexel founded the school as the Drexel Institute of Art, Science, and Industry to provide educational opportunities in the "practical arts and sciences" for men and women of all backgrounds. The school became commonly known as the Drexel Institute of Technology before achieving university status in 1970.

In 1918 Drexel established a cooperative educational program in which students spent periods of time working in the industry allied to their field of study. This gave them practical experience as well as a means of earning tuition for their next period of study. Companies liked the program because it provided above-average workers at a nominal cost. It also permitted them to make job offers to graduates who already had experience working with their companies. Drexel was not the first school to offer this program, but it now has one of the oldest, largest, and most successful such programs in the nation. More than 1,500 companies in 38 states and 11 countries participate in the program.

Drexel became the first university to require its students to have microcomputers, in the early 1980s, and *U.S. News and World Report* ranked its College of Information Science and Technology number one in the nation. Its Library and Information Science Program is similarly ranked in the top 10. Drexel each year graduates more than 1 percent of all graduating engineers in the country.

In 2002, Drexel merged with MCP Hahneman University. Hahneman had its origins in 1850 as the Female Medical College of Pennsylvania, the first medical school for women in the world. As a result, the Drexel University College of Medicine is the nation's largest private medical school.

September 1891— In this month the school that would become the California Institute of Technology (Caltech) was begun. The first step came when local businessman and politician/philanthropist Amos G. Throop rented the Wooster Block building in Pasadena, California. He founded a vocational school there, which he named Throop University. It opened in November 1891 to 31 students. The school went through successive names of Throop Polytechnic Institute and Throop College of Technology before becoming the California Institute of Technology in 1920.

The event that transformed the modest local school into one of national significance was the arrival of astronomer George Ellery Hale on Throop's board of trustees in 1907. Hale, who would become famous as the first director of the Mount Wilson Observatory (built a few years before near Pasadena) and for the discoveries he would make there, envisioned turning Throop's school into a first-class institution for engineering and scientific research and education.

Hale was able to attract private gifts of land and money to equip the school with modern laboratory facilities. In 1922, after the school had been renamed, Hale was able to attract prestigious scientists Arthur Noyes and Robert Millikan as faculty members and researchers. Caltech then entered a period of rapid growth. The Jet Propulsion Laboratory and the great observatory on Palomar Mountain were among the notable items that eventually grew out of Caltech. It also became famous for the work done there on particle physics.

Caltech remains a relatively small school, with 900 undergraduate and 1,200 graduate students. But 915 faculty members serve the school, and its list of winners of the Nobel Prize in various scientific disciplines is very impressive.

1892— During this year the Committee of Ten, headed by Charles William Eliot, president of Harvard University, convened a National Council on Education under the auspices of the National Education Association (NEA), and wrote a report on what the committee felt was the proper role of high schools in the United States. The committee was composed mostly of college presidents and professors, and they wanted to bring order to what they saw as a hodgepodge of suggested high school curricula. The committee wanted to standardize preparation for college, even if relatively few high school students went on to college at the time. The committee believed that all high school students should receive rigorous academic training regardless of their future college plans.

The conclusions of the Committee of Ten are quite similar to those of today regarding what subjects students should take in high school, but their approach was essentially overturned about a quarter of a century later by the issuance of the *Cardinal Principles of Secondary Education* in 1918 (see listing).

May 18, 1896— In what became an infamous decision, the Supreme Court of the United States announced that a Louisiana law requiring separate railway cars for blacks and whites was constitutional. The majority on the Court thus upheld state-imposed racial segregation. The case (*Plessy v. Ferguson*) was supposedly based on the "separate-but-equal" doctrine, but these words do not appear anywhere in the decision.

Plessy v. Ferguson was not an educational issue per se, but it led to or provided support for much subsequent segregation legislation in schools and elsewhere for the next 50 years. Justice Brown conceded that the intention of the Fourteenth Amendment was absolute equality for the races before the law. But Brown went on to say that "in the nature of things it could not have been intended to abolish distinctions based upon color, or to enforce social, as distinguished from political equality, or a commingling of the two races unsatisfactory to either."

The sense of the decision was that segregation does not in itself constitute unlawful discrimination. Analysts have noted that even 30 years after the end of the Civil War the Court felt the country was not ready for full equality between the races in the eyes of the law. It would take over another five decades before the Court would so rule (see entry for May 17, 1954).

1900— During this year, the College Entrance Examination Board was formed. The organization was set up by the presidents of 12 leading universities, and its function was to administer college admissions tests. The intent was to standardize the admissions process administratively and to force New England boarding schools to adopt a uniform curriculum. The first College Boards were conducted in 1901, using exams done in essay format for specific subject areas.

At the time the high school graduation rate was 6.4 percent (today it is about 68 percent, or 10 time as high). There were 106,000 students enrolled in public secondary schools, and progressives were beginning to call for less rote learning and for more lessons structured around the interests of students, in spite of the establishment of the College Boards.

April 20, 1901— A famous cartoon was first published in *Judge* magazine. It showed "Uncle Sam" pulling a "truant" along by his ear to the "Red, White, and Blue" schoolhouse named "Liberty School" where the teacher was named "Miss Columbia." The cartoon was a commentary on the concept of the times that educational leaders believed a prime function of schools was to transform immigrants and other "outsiders" into the images of what the educators believed a "true American" should be.

April 23, 1901— In Chicago, Anita McCormick Blaine founded the Colonel Francis W. Parker School for students from kindergarten through high school. The Parker School was one of the first to feature the ideas of the so-called "progressive movement" that began in the United States around 1900. The school offered education for the "whole individual" (mental, physical, and moral).

The school's namesake believed education should not be based on the "drilling method" that was generally used in schools of the time, but rather on the "learning by doing" method popular in the progressive movement. The progressive movement held that learning facts by rote was too limiting, and that children taught under the progressive method would develop into "active, democratic citizens and lifelong learners." Parker's proposals and John Dewey's research in the Chicago Laboratory School made the area a hotbed of progressive thought and practices, although there were a number of controversies later about how effective the progressive methods actually were. The Parker School, at least, still exists and is active in educational activities in the Chicago area.

Fall 1901— The oldest public "community college" began as an experimental postgraduate high school program in Joliet, Illinois. The program was developed by J. Stanley Brown, superintendent of Joliet Township High School, and William Rainey Harper, president of the University of Chicago. They created a "junior college" that academically paralleled the first two years of a four-year college or university. This permitted students to remain within their community and still pursue a college education.

By December 1902, the program had expanded to include students outside the specific high school district, and the board of trustees had made the courses available tuition free. In 1916 the program was officially named Joliet Junior College, and the idea had begun to spread across the nation. From an initial enrollment of six students in 1901, Joliet Community College has grown to 10,000 students today in courses for credit and to 21,000 students in noncredit courses. Nationwide, junior colleges today award two-year diplomas in a number of disciplines. They also usually permit, after two years, relatively easy entry to the upper classes of a regular four-year college for many students who would have never been able to enter a traditional four-year college directly from high school.

In total in the United States, about 1,000 community colleges exist today, and they serve nearly 12 million students. About 57 percent of the students are taking courses for college credit (almost seven million), with the remainder basically taking courses to expand their knowledge in specific areas.

July 28, 1903— Mary Harris, who would later be known as Mother Jones, led a caravan of poor children from the textile mills of Lexington, Pennsylvania, to the home of President Theodore Roosevelt in Oyster Bay, New York. The caravan was meant to call attention to the problem of child labor, especially the aspect that the children never got to go to school. The universalization of school access was not yet accepted everywhere in the United States, and the lack of an education doomed poor children to an ever-repeating cycle of poverty. Although the president refused to meet with the demonstrators, this "Children's Crusade" brought the issue of child labor and universal education to the attention of the public.

Mother Jones was 73 years old at the time, and to the end of her life of exactly 100 years, she agitated for a number of social issues in conjunction with labor unions. She was a very controversial figure, and in many levels of society she was considered infamous rather than famous. The magazine *Mother Jones* was named after the original Mary Harris, and it promotes many of the social issues espoused by its namesake.

June 28, 1904— Helen Keller became the first deaf and blind individual to receive a bachelor of arts degree, graduating cum laude from Radcliffe College, then a college that was essentially an annex for females at Harvard University. Harvard did not offer an education to females at the time, as only males were then permitted to attend Harvard. It would take over 300 years after its founding in 1636 before Harvard would admit female undergraduates.

The Radcliffe degree was the result of intensive work by Helen Keller and her constant companion and teacher, Anne Sullivan (see entry for March 3, 1887). It took them about 15 years to move through the Perkins Institute for the Blind in Boston, the Wright-Humason School for the Deaf in New York, and the Cambridge School for Young Ladies, a preparatory school for Radcliffe, and then Radcliffe itself.

By the time of her graduation, Helen Keller could write both in Braille and by using a conventional typewriter. She published the first of her many books, *The Story of My Life*, in 1903. In another decade, Helen Keller and Ann Sullivan began a career on the lecture circuit that lasted almost 50 years and encompassed a number of foreign countries. Helen Keller died at the age of 88 in 1968, a symbol of how an extremely productive life can be created from an almost hopeless beginning with education from dedicated teachers and an iron will from a student.

1905— During this year a French psychologist, Alfred Binet, was credited with inventing a test that would measure one's "intelligence." His intent was to help French school administrators predict a student's performance in school and identify slow learners. The basic test would be adapted in the United States about a decade later. It set off a still-controversial cycle of testing children for intelligence and led to creation of the Intelligence Quotient (IQ). (See listing for Lewis Terman, 1916.)

April 1905— The first bookmobile in the United States was introduced during this month via the Washington County Free Library in Hagerstown, Maryland. Mary Titcomb, the local librarian, had in 1904 started 66 "deposit stations" of 30 volumes each in general stores and post offices throughout the county so the rural population could have access to books. These deposit stations eventually became reading rooms and then branch libraries.

Titcomb decided in 1905 to take the books directly to rural homes. A wagon was built to hold 200 books, some on display shelves on the outside of the wagon. Led by a team of horses, the wagon covered 16 specific routes over about 500 square miles, with its farthest destination about four days away. The wagon was demolished at a rail crossing by a freight train in August 1910 (fortunately the driver survived), but in 1912 the wagon was replaced by a specially equipped International Harvester automobile. The bookmobile service was back in business with an improved transit time. Such services have been contributing to the education of adults and children throughout the United States ever since.

November 15, 1905— The trustees of the Carnegie Foundation for the Advancement of Teaching met in Andrew Carnegie's New York City mansion to discuss methods to improve education in colleges and high schools in the United States. These trustees included many university presidents who had great influence on educational practices in the nation. Carnegie had endowed the foundation with $10 million to provide pensions for retired college professors. One result of this meeting was the "Carnegie unit," which would become an important measuring stick for colleges and the high schools preparing students for college.

A Carnegie unit was defined in 1906 as a course of five periods weekly throughout an academic year on a subject suitable for secondary education. The periods evolved to be 50 to 55 minutes long. A college was defined as an institution having at least six fulltime professors offering a course of four full years in the liberal arts and sciences, and requiring four full years of academic or high school preparation. The Carnegie unit would be the measuring rod of time and credit for each subject, and at least 14 of these units would be required in a "true" college. The trustees also defined the preferred order of subjects to be mastered both in colleges and high schools. Most of these definitions are still with us today.

December 8, 1906— On this Saturday in 1906, a meeting of the Chicago Merchants Club listened to addresses delivered on the subject of "The Public Schools and Their Administration." It was an example of how public education reforms of the era were being directed by elite groups who were determined to bring "scientific management" to a reorganization of the educational system. In this way it as part of the "progressive reforms" initiated by the writings of John Dewey.

January 13, 1908— The Vocational Guidance Bureau of Boston opened its doors to its first young adults. Frank Parsons, a nationally known social and political reformer, founded the bureau. Parsons had founded the "Breadwinner's College" in Boston in 1905, and he was part of a reform movement to help ordinary citizens and recent immigrants gain educational opportunities. He even ran unsuccessfully for mayor of Boston in 1895, representing the Populist, Socialist, and Prohibition parties.

The Vocational Guidance Bureau was the first organized attempt to offer vocational and counseling services to young adults. It is considered to have laid the foundation for the American counseling movement that followed. Decades later, counselors in high schools to help students choose and apply for entrance to appropriate colleges were common, but it was not common when Parsons began his pioneering work.

Parsons was able to convince many prominent citizens to serve on the board of trustees of the bureau, and as a result there was no fee for the services offered by the bureau. The statement by Parsons that the purpose of the bureau was "to aid young people in choosing an occupation, preparing themselves for it, finding an opening in the chosen field, and building up a career of efficacy and success" is one that is relevant even a century later in the field of counseling.

1909— During this year, junior high schools were established in Columbus, Ohio, and in Berkeley, California. Other cities soon followed. This was part of an organizational concept to divide elementary and secondary schools into six-year blocks, so that six years in elementary school would be followed by junior high school and senior high school in a 6–3–3 arrangement. After 1930, junior high schools became common in the United States.

February 12, 1909— The organization that would become the National Association for the Advancement of Colored People (NAACP) was founded by W. E. DuBois and others. The NAACP, originally called the National Negro Committee, would become the legal focus of actions during the rest of the first half of the twentieth century to achieve desegregation in public schools, a goal finally reached in 1954 in the *Brown v. Board of Education* decision (see entry).

1909—*How We Think*, by John Dewey, was published during this year (some references give the release date as 1910). The book presents the basis for Dewey's emphasis on "learning by doing" as the best method to educate children. Dewey was considered by many as a key element in the progressive movement in education during the first half of the twentieth century. But many analysts point out that Dewey's writings were hard to follow, and thus his ideas were difficult to put into practice, especially as he actually intended them to be implemented.

The Laboratory School which Dewey and his wife, Alice, founded at the University of Chicago around 1901, became a subject of dispute in 1904, and Dewey moved on to New York City to become a professor at Columbia for the next three decades. But the famous Lincoln School he founded in Manhattan quickly failed. Thus, although Dewey was regarded as an important source of ideas about "progressivism," relatively few of his proposed reforms actually were put into practice to a significant degree during his long lifetime.

1912 — Edward Thorndike's book *Education, A First Book* was published during this year. Thorndike was a professor of educational psychology at Columbia University, and he stressed the difference between what he called "personal teaching" by instruction and what a student could gain from reading a textbook. Thorndike's book was considered to be a part of the new "progressive" approach to education. Thorndike proposed in a sense what would become "programmed instruction." He stated that "If, by a miracle of mechanical ingenuity, a book could be so arranged that only to him who had done what was directed on page one would page two become visible, and so on, much that now requires personal instruction could be managed by print."

1916 — *Democracy and Education*, by John Dewey, was published during this year. In this book Dewey attempted to expand upon and modify the ideas of Rousseau and Plato relative to education. Dewey, who was credited with playing a key role in the development of what was known as "progressive education," felt it was important that "education not be the teaching of dead facts, but that the skills and knowledge which students learned be fully integrated into their lives as citizens and human beings." Dewey's ideas were generally popular with educators, but some critic stated that these ideas were "never broadly and deeply integrated into the practices of American public schools." This idea is reinforced in the entry about Dewey in 1909.

1916 — Lewis Terman published *The Measurement of Intelligence* during this year. Terman, a professor of education and psychology at Stanford from 1910 to 1946 who became the president of the American Psychological Association in 1923, introduced the Stanford-Binet intelligence test in this book. (The original Binet intelligence test was developed in France in 1905 — see listing.) Terman also incorporated William Stern's development of the "intelligence quotient" or IQ, in which the intellectual ability score or mental age is divided by the chronological age to get a ratio. The Stanford version of the test became widely used in the United States as a forecast of academic achievement. The term IQ has been a lightning rod for much controversy. Although IQ objectively appears to meet its intended goal of forecasting which students are most likely to succeed in higher education, its use (and often misapplication) has created a cadre of people who feel the test is prejudiced against immigrants and ethnic minorities.

Terman was asked by the United States military in World War I to help develop a test to determine what functions and duties best suited the new recruits pouring into the Army. The eventual result, in conjunction with work done by Harvard professor Robert Yerkes, was the so-called Alpha and Beta tests, the Beta test being an effort to measure ability in illiterate and foreign-language soldiers. The Stanford Achievement Test grew out of this work, and the concept of testing all schoolchildren for their "IQ" also followed. Even with much attendant controversy, the practice is still widely used.

1917— The vocational education movement was given a big boost by passage of the federal Smith-Hughes Act during this year. The act provided federal aid for the states by helping to pay the salaries of vocational teachers in high schools, and it aided the institutions that trained such teachers.

Vocational Guidance Bureaus had been opened earlier in the decade (see entry for January 13, 1908), and the progressive movement being pushed by John Dewey (see entry for 1909) all combined to make vocational/manual education popular in this period, and the Smith-Hughes Act helped vocational training reach new heights.

1918— During this year a new group of high school reformers under the name of the Commission on the Reorganization of Secondary Education (which had been appointed five years earlier) issued a new paper on what they saw as the purpose of high school. As had been the Committee of Ten in 1892 (see listing), this group was under the auspices of the National Education Association (NEA), but they reached a completely different conclusion than the Committee of Ten. The new group titled their report *Cardinal Principles of Education*, and they took the position that high schools should prepare students for their various future positions in life, which in most cases did not include a college education.

This position supported the use of intelligence and tracking tests designed to discover what fields students were best suited for in life after high school. The *Cardinal Principles* saw high school as a final educational process rather than a preparation for postsecondary education. This was yet another entry in the apparently never-ending battle over what students should learn in high school. The *Cardinal Principles* report was published by the United States Bureau of Education and became the basic outline for the role of high schools in the nation until the advent of *Sputnik* in 1957 caused a dramatic change in outlook once more (see entry for October 8, 1957).

March 15, 1919 — The Progressive Education Association (PEA) was formed in Washington, D.C., by educators Marietta Johnson, Eugene R. Smith, and Stanwood Cobb. Charles W. Eliot of Harvard agreed to serve as honorary president to lend prestige to the association. The journal *Progressive Education* appeared in 1924. The early members were primarily people associated with private schools, and the ideas of John Dewey were foremost among the recommendations of the PEA.

Many analysts claim the primary job of the PEA was to sell the concept of progressivism to teachers in the nation's schools. There were 10,000 association members by the late 1930s, including many public school personnel. There was a sense in the country at the time the association was formed that school reform of some sort was needed due to the difficulty schools had been having educating the many immigrants pouring into the country in the previous decades. But specific reforms identified as "progressivism" were hard to define, and the association soon broke into different camps with different agendas.

The association died in 1955, just before the launch of *Sputnik* in 1957 solidified the clamor for teaching of "harder" subjects in school and made it an overwhelming demand. In general, progressivism was seen as "soft."

May 23, 1919 — The California Legislature agreed to establish in Los Angeles a "southern" branch of the University of California, then located only in the northern part of the state in Berkeley. In 1927, the southern branch was renamed the University of California at Los Angeles, or UCLA.

UCLA had its start as the Los Angeles State Normal School, opened on August 29, 1882, to train teachers for the growing population of Southern California. The constant growth of the school led Director Ernest Moore to petition in 1917 for the school to become the second campus of the University of California, and this request was granted two years later. By then the Normal School had 1,500 students.

UCLA grew steadily together with the region it served, and it added new courses of study until it was one of the largest and most diverse universities in the nation. It became especially noted for its School of Medicine, which started in 1946 when enrollment at the university reached 13,800, almost 10 times as large as it was when UCLA began in 1919. The UCLA Medical Center is now one of the top such facilities in the country, and in the world. The first open-heart surgery in the western United States was performed here in 1956.

UCLA is now a megauniversity with nearly 40,000 students, and is one of the most desirable destinations for college-bound students in a very wide range of academic disciplines. It also leads the nation in the number of NCAA Division I sports championships, going past a total of 91 in 2004.

February 1921— In a series of meetings held during this month (after a similar series held in the middle of 1920), the American Association of Junior Colleges was formed. The name was changed over the years to the American Association of Community Colleges. In 1930, the association began publishing its own journal, now known as the *Community College Journal.* As noted previously, the present nationwide population of community colleges had its origin in Joliet, Illinois, in 1901 (see entry for Fall 1901). There are nearly 1,000 community colleges in the United States today, serving about 12 million students.

1922— During this year, the Ruggles Street School and Training Center was opened in Boston by Abigail Adams Eliot and Mrs. Henry Greeneleaf Pearson. It was one of the first nursery schools in the United States, and was a natural training ground for preschool teachers as well as a research center for observing the development of young children.

In 1926 the school became the Nursery Training School of Boston, and in 1951 it became associated with Tufts University. Then teachers at the school were able to pursue a college education at the same time as they taught at the school. Such schools, of which the Ruggles School was one of the first, are often known as "laboratory schools" because the prime objective was to train teachers and observe child development in an actual setting rather than to simply provide a suitable school setting for children who are two to four years old.

June 4, 1923— The United States Supreme Court announced that a Nebraska law forbidding the teaching of modern foreign languages to grade-school children was unconstitutional. The stated purpose of the law was to promote assimilation and civic development. But the use of the law to prosecute a man teaching German in a Lutheran school at the request of parents in a time of "peace and tranquility" violated the due process clause (Fourteenth Amendment) of the constitution.

It is probable that the unspoken intention of the law was to prohibit the teaching of German while anti-German feelings still ran high following World War I. This ruling struck down that process in a way that was relatively unemotional.

June 1, 1925— The United States Supreme Court announced its decision in a case challenging an Oregon law requiring parents of children between the ages of eight and 16 to send their children only to public school in the district in which the children resided. This law was challenged by the Society of the Sisters of the Holy Names of Jesus and Mary, a parochial school. The Court agreed unanimously that the Oregon law was unconstitutional because "the fundamental liberty upon which all governments in this Union repose excludes any general power of the state to standardize its children by forcing them to accept instruction from public teachers only."

This decision was a major victory for parochial schools throughout the United States, upholding their right to establish and maintain school systems.

July 10, 1925 — What became known as the "Scopes Monkey Trial" opened in Dayton, Tennessee. The trial was essentially created as a publicity stunt to attract attention to the town of Dayton, which had dwindled in population to 1,800 from 3,000 over the past 30 years. The followers of Populist William Jennings Bryan, who was a three-time Democratic candidate for president (and three times a loser — in 1896, 1900, and 1908), had managed to get legislation introduced in 15 states to ban the teaching of evolution in schools. In February 1925 Tennessee had enacted such a bill.

The American Civil Liberties Union (ACLU) had advertised that it would offer its services to anyone challenging the new Tennessee statue. Several town leaders, including the superintendent of schools, got a science teacher named John Scopes to agree to stand trial for teaching evolution. Two local attorneys, who were friends of Scopes, agreed to prosecute. The group actually hoped to overturn the new law, but their primary purpose was to attract attention (and visitors) to the town of Dayton. As it turned out, they succeeded beyond their wildest dreams in terms of attracting attention.

The publicity generated by the announcement of the trail and the involvement of the ACLU got William Jennings Bryan himself to offer to help the prosecution. Soon, famous retired defense lawyer Clarence Darrow, now approaching 70, offered to help the defense. A clearly carnival atmosphere surrounded Dayton as the opening of the trial neared. Lemonade stands were doing a brisk business in the hot Tennessee summer, while banners decorated the streets of the town. Chimpanzees performed in a sideshow on Main Street. It was said they were going to testify for the prosecution. A serious issue was going to be debated, but the atmosphere in which the debate would take place was anything but serious.

The trial itself featured Darrow calling Bryan to the stand to testify as an expert witness on the Bible. Darrow had planned to call expert witnesses on evolution, but was rebuffed by the judge. The press of the day wrote that Darrow "won" the debate by making Bryan finally appear unsure and foolish. But the trial ended with Darrow requesting a guilty verdict so he could appeal the decision to higher courts and attempt to get the anti-evolution statute overturned on constitutional grounds. The jury delivered such a verdict in eight minutes and the judge ordered Scopes fined $100, the minimum amount allowable. Darrow's clever tactic precluded Bryan from giving a closing speech, which he had worked on for days. But the appeal to the Tennessee Supreme Court did not have the desired effect. The court reversed the verdict 18 months later on January 14, 1927, on the grounds that the jury, not the judge, should have set the fine. Then the Supreme Court dismissed the case. The statute was not reversed on constitutional grounds.

It would not be until 43 years later, in 1968, that the United States Supreme Court would find such laws unconstitutional. But even today, disputes are still going on in this area. The famous Dayton Monkey Trial ended with no real resolution in its day, and 80 years later the specific issue continues to be the subject of controversy. The general issue of what should and what should not be taught in the schools will likely continue to be debated permanently.

1926— The Scholastic Aptitude Test (SAT) was given to high school students for the first time. The author of the test, Carl Brigham, had worked on the Army IQ tests with Robert Yerkes during World War I (see entry for 1916), and had published a book titled *A Study of American Intelligence* based on the results of the testing. In his book Brigham analyzed the results by race and determined that American education was declining and would do so at an accelerating rate as the "racial mixture becomes more and more extensive." This, of course, was during a time when blacks in the South (and many other places) received their educations in segregated schools.

Brigham administered his own versions of the Army tests to Princeton (see listing) freshmen and to applicants to Cooper Union College (see listing) in New York, and the College Board (see listing) put him in charge of a committee to develop a test that could be used by a wider group of schools. That test became the SAT.

1927— During this year seven women's colleges met to create an organization to promote private, independent women's colleges and the premise of "separate but equal" liberal arts education for women. The colleges were Barnard, Bryn Mawr, Mount Holyoke, Radcliffe, Smith, Vassar, and Wellesley (see listings for each). Although Mount Holyoke could trace its roots to 1837, it did not officially become a college until 1888. The rest of the colleges were founded between 1865 and 1893 in the northeastern United States. By 1927 they were among the most prestigious colleges for women in the country, and all had exacting admission standards and impressive reputations for providing a very high-quality education.

These colleges became popularly known as the Seven Sisters, a term intended to associate them in the public's mind with the eight prestigious Ivy League schools for men, also located in the northeastern United States

(Harvard, Yale, Princeton, Pennsylvania, Columbia, Brown, Dartmouth, and Cornell), but the term Ivy League really did not become generally used until 1937 (see listing for each school and the Ivy League). However, except for Cornell (founded in 1865), all of the Ivy League colleges were founded before the Revolutionary War, and long were among the most prestigious in the nation. But again except for Cornell, women were not accepted at Ivy League schools as undergraduates.

Barnard College had a prior association with Columbia since around 1900, and Radcliffe had an association with Harvard since 1889, but neither Columbia nor Harvard admitted women as undergraduates (Harvard did so in 1970 and Columbia in 1983). When all the Ivy League colleges became coeducational by the 1970s and 1980s (as noted, Cornell had been coeducational since its founding in 1865), these special relationships changed. Also, the basic reason for having women's colleges, to offer educational opportunities that men's colleges would not, changed as well (Vassar, for example, became a coeducational college in 1969). Some women feel there still is value in offering women an education in an environment consisting only of other women, but such colleges could be on shaky legal ground if challenged because the "separate but equal" concept was thrown out by the Supreme Court in its famous desegregation ruling in 1954 (and afterwards).

November 1, 1927— The Mildred Rosalie Wimpfheimer Nursery School day nursery was opened at Vassar College (see entry for September 26, 1865). The nursery school was donated by Charles A. Wimpfheimer in honor of his daughter's graduation from Vassar with the class of 1927.

This nursery school was another in the line of "laboratory schools" that were intended both to serve as a setting to train teachers and to observe the development of children in the range of two to four years of age. Other well-known schools of this type were established at the State University of Iowa; the Teachers College at Columbia University; and Smith College for Women (a school similar to Vassar in educating only women).

There were also "laboratory schools" associated with major universities that followed children all the way from nursery school through high school. Examples of these schools were located at the University of Chicago, the University of Michigan, and the University of California at Los Angeles (UCLA).

1930— As of this year there were still 130,000 one-room schools operating in the United States. Their number dwindled to almost zero as the century progressed.

April 28, 1930— Chief Justice Charles Hughes of the United States Supreme Court delivered the opinion of the Court concerning an issue raised in Louisiana contending that the application of a tax to supply free textbooks to the children of the state was unconstitutional because some children used the textbooks in religious and other sectarian schools. The Supreme Court of Louisiana had found the process permissible, and the United States Supreme Court effectively upheld that decision.

Justice Hughes stated that the true beneficiaries of the process were the children of the state. No specific schools were identified as recipients, and all children were to benefit from the process without any form of discrimination based on race, color, ethnic origin, or religion. The schools in which the children used the books were irrelevant to the intent of the process, which was to provide textbooks to all children of the state free of charge. The Supreme Court, as did the lower court, found no harm to the Constitution in the process.

April 1930— Eleanor Roosevelt had her article "Good Citizenship: The Purpose of Education" published in the issue of *Pictorial Review* carrying this date. In this article Mrs. Roosevelt noted the conventional answer of acquiring knowledge, then went further, citing a recent statement by the archbishop of York: "the true purpose of education is to produce good citizens."

In the text of the article, Mrs. Roosevelt recalled that she received a typical education for the girls of her day, but she was ashamed to admit that when she was 20 years old she was asked by an Englishwoman how the government of the United States functioned, and Mrs. Roosevelt was embarrassed to have to say she had no idea. And although much had changed since she was a girl, there was still much to do to develop informed and intelligent citizens, and to make them aware that everyone is responsible for "the trend of thought and the action of our times."

She concluded by saying that the standards of citizenship our schools and we instill in our children will determine the success of our national experiment in government "by the people, for the people."

September 8, 1931— In the issue of *The Nation's Schools* carrying this date, a Missouri educator named W. W. Carpenter wrote an article titled "Is the Educational Utopia in Sight?" He was not being sarcastic even though the Great Depression was just beginning. Carpenter's answer to his question was a resounding "yes." He believed at the time that Americans were making steady progress toward the goal of giving every child an appropriate education. He went on to state "we are carrying on the most important experiment in democracy the world has ever seen, the results of which may determine educational procedures for centuries to come." His opinion was representative of educators in this era. They felt educational progress was being made and better education would lead to a better society.

1933— In this year the use of the Scholastic Aptitude Test (SAT — see listing for 1926) started its trend toward becoming universal, after James Conant was appointed president of Harvard University. Conant and his two assistants, Henry Chauncy and Wilbur Bender, had the task of finding a way to select public school students for a Harvard Scholarship program. The three men traveled to Princeton (see listing) in 1933 to meet Carl Brigham, inventor of the SAT.

Starting in 1934, the SAT was used to select students for Harvard Scholarships. A year later, Harvard required all general candidates for the school to take the SAT. In the same year, IBM machines were developed to score tests for the New York State Regents and the Providence, Rhode Island, public schools. By the end of the decade, the SAT was used as a scholarship test for all Ivy League schools (see listing).

1936— Maria Montessori published *The Secret of Childhood* during this year. In this book Montessori discussed her extensive research and observations about child behavior, and a new way of approaching the education of children. She stated that the proper environment must be established to stimulate the "liberation" of a child's hidden characteristics and to permit the child to flourish. This theory fit well with other progressive child-centered theories developed in the United States during the first part of the twentieth century.

Montessori was born in Italy and was the first female Italian physician in the modern era. She opened her first school in Rome on January 6, 1907, after being assigned the task of trying to educate the "idiots" and "uneducable" in the city. She was exiled to India by Mussolini during World War II, and lived in the Netherlands until she died in 1952 at the age of 82. The Association Montessori Internationale (AMI) is still headquartered in the Netherlands.

There was much interest in the Montessori method in the United States in the 1910s, but it later waned. In 1960 Nancy McCormick Rambusch established the American Montessori Society and there was a revival of interest in the approach.

October 14, 1937— Caswell Adams, a sportswriter for the *New York Herald Tribune*, complained about being assigned to cover a football game between the University of Pennsylvania and Columbia University. He said he was tired of watching "the ivy grow every Saturday afternoon," and he wanted to see some football away from the "ivy-covered halls of learning." Fellow (and famous) sportswriter Stanley Woodward overheard the complaint and coined the term "Ivy League," using it in one of his very popular columns. The phrase caught on and ever since has been used to describe the eight prestigious (and very old) universities of the Northeast. These include (in order of their founding) Harvard University in Cambridge, Massachusetts (founded 1636); Yale University in New Haven, Connecticut (1701); Princeton University in Princeton, New Jersey (1746); University of Pennsylvania in Philadelphia (1751); Columbia University in New York City (1754); Brown University in Providence, Rhode Island (1764); Dartmouth College in Hanover, New Hampshire (1769); and Cornell University in Ithaca, New York (1865). Thus, all but Cornell were founded during the colonial era, and the schools have often been called the "Ancient Eight."

The term "Ivy League" referred originally to the various sports associations formed by the schools, but it is now used in reference to the common high academic standards of the schools, and an "Ivy League" education is considered among the most desirable in the United States, if not the most desirable. February 1954 is often taken as the formal starting date of the Ivy League. On that date the schools substantially de-emphasized sports in terms of competition with outside schools in favor of competition among just the Ivy League schools. There were agreements on the degree to which sports would be subsidized by the schools and the academic standards athletes had to meet. Previously the Ivy League schools were among the best — and oldest — sports teams in the country. But by 1956 spring football practice was eliminated and the old form of athletic scholarships was banned. Thus, although all sports can be part of an Ivy League education, the emphasis is on academic performance, and there are no "dumb jock" stereotypes at an Ivy League school.

It should be noted that the story the Ivy League name grew out of a sports association formed almost a century ago among Harvard, Yale, Columbia, and Princeton called the "Four League" is not true. The use of the Roman numeral IV for four is supposedly to have led to the term "Ivy League." But like most popular myths of this type, this one is also untrue.

1938— During this year President Roosevelt signed the Fair Labor Standards Act prohibiting children under 16 from working during school hours.

1938— The case of Lloyd Gaines versus the State of Missouri decided during this year gave the National Association for the Advancement of Colored People (NAACP), led by Charles Hamilton Houston, a big victory in its strategy of forcing law schools to create costly "separate but equal" facilities for blacks and whites under the "separate but equal" doctrine, or be forced to integrate their schools.

The NAACP was not yet trying to overturn the "separate but equal" doctrine but rather was trying to force schools to effectively abandon it rather than build the facilities necessary to maintain it. In 1938, the University of Missouri was ordered by the United States Supreme Court to furnish Lloyd Gaines, a black seeking admission to law school, "within its borders facilities for legal education substantially equal to those which the state there offered for the persons of the white race, whether or not other Negroes sought the same opportunity." It was a precedent the NAACP realized would force other states to integrate or build. There would be attempts to "integrate" in a limited fashion, but the stage was set for postsecondary integration of educational facilities.

May 1938— *The Behavior of Organisms*, by psychologist B. F. Skinner, was published in this month. Among other disciplines, the book eventually had a strong impact on the process of education and teaching. The research cited in the book was based on Skinner's work with white rats and how they were conditioned to press a lever (the "operant") to obtain something desirable like food. Later Skinner would do similar work with pigeons, and condition them to perform certain tasks by pecking in the proper way. He emphasized the idea of positive reinforcement to achieve a certain behavior.

Skinner eventually wrote a number of books, and he worked extensively on education and programmed instruction. His book *Verbal Behavior* was published in 1957. Skinner received many honors in his career, but was also the target of savage attacks by some groups. He proposed the use of what came to be known as a "Skinner box" in helping to train young children, and used one to some extent on his own daughter. Some people felt Skinner was too radical and tended to treat humans like any other animal. But the idea of reinforcing desirable behavior is behind many educational techniques that do not explicitly state this concept.

1943— During this year the Gallaudet School, for the deaf (see entry for 1864), gained fame in sports as its "Five Iron Men" won the Mason-Dixon Conference basketball championship. Gallaudet also supposedly originated the football "huddle" when its team discovered that opposing teams were reading their signals delivered in sign language and essentially decoding their plays.

April 2, 1943— The Army-Navy College Qualifying Test was administered to over 316,000 high school seniors all over the nation. This proved that standardized multiple-choice tests could be given to a mass group.

The next month, in May, President James Conant of Harvard published the third in a series of articles for the *Atlantic Monthly* entitled "Wanted: American Radicals." Conant's view was that the American radical "believes in equality of opportunity, not equality of rewards."

June 14, 1943— The United States Supreme Court announced that a West Virginia law requiring public school students to salute the flag on pain of being declared "insubordinate," and punished by expulsion and charges of delinquency if they refused, was unconstitutional. The Court held that the salute was a form of speech and a means of communicating ideas. Thus, its compulsion was a violation of the First Amendment free speech clause and was unconstitutional.

This ruling overturned prior rulings, which took an opposite view. Justice Robert Jackson argued that "no official, high or petty, can prescribe what shall be orthodox in politics, nationalism, religion, or other matters of opinion or force citizens to confess by word or act their faith therein."

June 22, 1944— The Servicemen's Readjustment Act of 1944 was signed into law by President Franklin D. Roosevelt. It was coined as the "GI Bill of Rights" by an American Legion publicist, and later became simply the "GI Bill." The act had an effect on college education that was far beyond what was anticipated at the time of its passage.

The act was basically intended to reduce the possibility of a postwar depression brought on by the widespread unemployment that might result when 15 million men and women serving in the armed services entered the workforce when the war ended. After suffering through the Great Depression of the 1930s, which had ended only when World War II began and mobilized the civilian workforce, the nation was trying to avoid a new depression when the war ended. The act was intended to help returning service men and women adjust to civilian life in the areas of hospitalization, the buying of homes and businesses, and the acquisition of any education necessary to make the returning veterans more employable.

The GI Bill provided tuition, living expenses, books and supplies, equipment, and counseling services for veterans to continue their education at every level. Not only did veterans take advantage of these provisions in great numbers, schools began to organize to provide the needed services and thus gain much-needed sources of revenue. In the next seven years, over 8 million veterans received the educational benefits. About 2.3 million attended schools and colleges, 3.5 million received school training, and 3.4 million received on-the-job training. The number of degrees awarded by colleges and universities more than doubled between 1940 and 1950, and the percentage of Americans with bachelor degrees or higher increased from 4.6 percent in 1945 to 25 percent a half-century later. The GI Bill essentially established the concept of the benefits of going to college throughout the population well beyond the elite few who normally went on to college.

When the bill expired in 1956, a total of $14.5 billion had been disbursed. But the Veterans Administration estimated that the increase in income taxes paid by the highly educated veterans repaid the cost of the bill several times over. Further, with the aid of the GI Bill, veterans bought 20 percent of all new homes built after the war, sending positive effects rippling through the economy. Colleges and universities added staff, buildings, courses, and equipment to service the demands for education by the veterans. The GI Bill was extended to help veterans during the Korean War era and the Vietnam era with similar positive effects. The field of education was fundamentally and permanently altered in a positive way by the GI Bill.

August 1945— During this month, Harvard University issued the report *General Education in a Free Society*, which soon became popularly known as the "Redbook." The report addressed an issue that had been debated for decades and one which would continue to be debated even after the new millennium. That issue was what curriculum in high school would strike the proper balance between the needs of students planning to go to college and the needs of students planning to go no further in their education than high school.

At the time of the report, only about 25 percent of high school graduates went on to college (the percentage today is near 65 percent). Thus, the report concluded that the prime job of high schools is to prepare students for "citizenship in a free society." The age of this issue can be judged by considering the fact that those on one side were called Jeffersonian and those on the other were called Jacksonian.

Thomas Jefferson believed the prime purpose of education was to screen the "rubble" and find the gifted students who should be trained for leadership in their specialties and who would thus lead the nation. Jefferson assumed only male leaders would be found via this process. Andrew Jackson believed education should concentrate on raising the average level of the masses.

The Harvard report came down on the Jacksonian side of the issue (as did a report also issued in 1945 called the "Prosser Resolution," by Charles Prosser, director of the Federal Board for Vocational Education), but this would all change after *Sputnik* in 1957 and *A Nation at Risk* in 1983 shocked the nation into realizing that it was falling behind other countries in science and math. This brought a demand for more "hard" subjects in high school and less "fluff."

January 1, 1948— A new testing agency, Educational Testing Service (ETS), officially opened for business in Princeton, New Jersey. Henry Chauncey was named president, and James Conant was named chairman of the board. The same year a branch office was established in Berkeley, California, to initiate a relationship with the University of California and hopefully to convince them to adopt the SAT as a requirement.

March 8, 1948— The Supreme Court of the United States decided that the use of public school system resources in Champaign, Illinois, to support classes in religion violated the establishment clause of the First Amendment and was unconstitutional. The classes were offered by various religious groups, and the fact that students were released for a time from their duty to attend school if they opted to take the various religious courses, clearly violated the First Amendment, in the opinion of the court.

After this opinion, the rest of the century would find the court often being asked to rule in similar cases, and except for some very narrow circumstances, the court would find in favor of those requesting practices involving religion in almost any way to be thrown out of public schools.

1948— Another crack in the wall of segregation was made during this year when the United States Supreme Court ruled that Lois Ada Riggs, a black woman, could not be denied entrance to a state law school in Oklahoma solely because of her race. This ruling confirmed that denial of entrance to a public school due to race only was unconstitutional.

June 5, 1950— The Supreme Court of the United States dealt another blow to the concept of "separate but equal" college facilities for blacks and whites. The Court announced that a Texas law forbidding admission of a black man to the University of Texas Law School and proposing "separate but equal" accommodations instead, was unconstitutional.

The Court found that the proposed "separate but equal" facility was unequal in a number of areas, but it found further that even the mere separation from the majority of law students harmed the students' abilities to compete in the legal arena. This made the law a violation of the equal protection clause of the Fourteenth Amendment and thus unconstitutional.

In a similar ruling made against the University of Oklahoma in 1950, the Court found that requiring a black student to sit in separate sections or in spaces adjacent to the classroom, library, and cafeteria was unconstitutional because such restrictions interfered with the student's "ability to study, to engage in discussions, and exchange views with other students, and, in general, to learn his craft." This ruling came very close to saying that the only "equal" facility was an integrated facility.

1951— During this year, another follow-up of "Terman's Kids" was conducted. This was a group of about 800 men selected from about 1,528 grade-school students in California in the early 1920s by Lewis Terman (see entry for 1916). The original group of students had IQ scores above 140. The average was 150, and 80 had scores of 170 or higher (in the general public, only about 15 percent of test subjects have an IQ above 116).

Most of the follow-up focused on the about 800 men who had gone into professional fields (this criteria tended to eliminate women because they did not normally go into professional fields in time periods shortly after the 1920s). By 1950, at an average age of 40, these 800 men had written and published 67 books, over 1,400 articles, 200 plays and short stories, and obtained over 150 patents. Seventy-eight had received a PhD, 48 an MD and 85 an LLB. Seventy-four were university professors, and 47 were listed in *American Men of Science*. As Terman noted, "nearly all of these numbers are 10 to 30 times as large as would be found for 800 men picked at random." The subject of IQ testing may be controversial, but this longitudinal study confirms that a high IQ is certainly predictive of future academic prowess.

When "Terman's Kids" reached their 70s, they were compared with the average person of that age, and were found to be healthier, happier, and richer. They also had a far lower incidence of suicide, alcoholism, and divorce. The studies were also felt to show that the thought that genius is closely related to insanity is a myth. Far fewer of Terman's group suffered from serious behavioral disorders when compared with the average populace.

1951— During this year, David Abraham of the Perkins Howe Press at the Perkins School for the Blind (see entry for 1829) finished development of the first Perkins Brailler. To date, over 280,000 Perkins Braillers have been produced and distributed to over 170 countries worldwide. Even in the age of the computer, the relatively simple and very reliable Perkins Brailler (which requires no electricity) is the preferred method for writing in Braille, especially in poorer areas of the world. The Brailler makes it possible for blind people to write as well as to read in Braille.

Louis Braille, a French teenager who became blind due to an accident at the age of three, developed the reading and writing system for the blind that bears his name in the early 1820s. Braille adapted a system used by the French military for "night writing," a system of 12 raised dots on paper that carried a message that could be read by soldiers at night without using lights. Braille used only six dots and created a method of making Braille reading material using a "slate" and a "stylus" in which each dot is created from the back of the page, writing in mirror image. Blind children can be taught quickly to "read" Braille, but few can master the art of writing in Braille in such a way.

Many attempts were made to create a Braillewriter in the 125 years after Braille created his system, but all were hard to use and easily broken. Frank Hall invented a kind of typewriter for Braille writing in 1892, and nearly all designs since that date followed his method; but costs, the need for frequent repairs, and noise were all objectionable.

A Perkins employee named David Abraham designed a better Braillewriter in the 1930s, but when it was ready to be tested in production in 1941, World War II caused a shortage of materials. When the materials became available in 1946, it took another five years to set up production and satisfy Abraham that the design was finalized. With some trepidation, Perkins began production. They had sunk considerable funds in the development of the machine, and if it was not popular, those funds would never be recovered. But the machine was an "instant" (after nearly 20 years of effort) success, and blind children could learn to fully communicate, writing in Braille as easily as learning to type.

February 28, 1951—The *Brown v. Board of Education* lawsuit was filed in federal district court in Kansas. When this case finally reached the United States Supreme Court, it was consolidated with several similar lawsuits to determine the constitutionality of segregation in public schools (see May 17, 1954 entry).

May 1951—The public school segregation case called *Briggs et al. v. Eliott et al.* went to trial in South Carolina. In this case Thurgood Marshall and the National Association for the Advancement of Colored People (NAACP) presented evidence showing that segregation itself was harmful to black schoolchildren in spite of any "separate but equal" considerations. The evidence included sociologist Kenneth Clark's controversial "doll study."

Kenneth Clark was a black psychologist who graduated from the City College of New York and was the first black to receive a PhD in psychology from Columbia University (his wife Mamie was the second). The couple developed a "doll test" that grew out of Mamie's master's degree thesis. In this test, black elementary school students were asked several questions about two dolls that were identical except for color. A large majority of the black students preferred the white doll, even when asked to identify the doll that looks most "like you." The white doll was consistently labeled the "nice doll" and the black doll the "bad doll." Kenneth Clark claimed this showed how blacks were given a sense of inferiority by segregation, but there was strident disagreement on the other side.

The District Court Judge refused to order desegregation of the school district but instead ordered the "equalization" of black schools there. The case moved on toward the United States Supreme Court.

June 1951—*Brown v. Board of Education* moved into trial in Kansas during this month. In August the District Court ruled that there was no "willful, intentional, or substantial discrimination" in Topeka's schools. Further, the court found that white and black school facilities were substantially equal, and that recent court decisions finding harm in simply separating the races applied only to graduate education. The case moved inexorably toward the United States Supreme Court.

1952— During this year, the present structure of questions for the verbal section of the SAT was established: reading comprehension, analogies, antonyms, and sentence completion questions.

April 1952— For the first time, in a Delaware public school segregation case, the court ruled that the black children were being denied equal protection under the law and that they should immediately be admitted to white schools. This time, the school district appealed the decision, and this case also moved toward the United States Supreme Court.

June 1952— The United States Supreme Court announced it would hear arguments in two of the key segregation cases in October 1952. One was the "Brown" case of Kansas and the other was the "Briggs" case of South Carolina.

July 16, 1952— President Truman signed the Veteran's Readjustment Assistance Act of 1952. It was also known as the Korean Conflict Bill, Public Law 550, and it provided benefits to Korean veterans in a manner similar to that of the original "GI Bill" passed in 1944. Once more the bill was a great boon to education. The "Korean Bill" offered more limited benefits and had more restrictions, but it continued the concept of helping returning veterans to receive a good education at government cost.

October 1952— Just days before arguments were to begin in the two selected segregation cases the United States Supreme Court had agreed to hear, the Court announced a postponement. Three weeks later, the Court announced it would also hear the Delaware cases, the District of Columbia case, and the case from Prince Edward County in Virginia. The fact the Court would hear all five school desegregation cases collectively showed that segregation was a truly national issue.

December 1952— From December 9 through December 11 the first round of arguments were held in the five combined school segregation cases being heard by the United States Supreme Court.

June 1953— In this month, the United States Supreme Court ordered that a second round of arguments in the five combined public school segregation cases be held in October 1953.

September 8, 1953— Fred Vinson, Jr., chief justice of the United States Supreme Court, died suddenly of a heart attack. President Eisenhower nominated California Governor Earl Warren to replace Vinson as interim chief on September 30. The Court rescheduled arguments in the five combined public school segregation cases until December 1953.

Justice Warren would eventually deliver the unanimous ruling in the segregation cases, and was considered a prime architect of that ruling.

December 1953— From December 7 until December 9, the second round of arguments in the five combined public school desegregation cases was heard before the United States Supreme Court.

March 1954— In this month the Senate confirmed Earl Warren as chief justice of the United States Supreme Court. The stage was now set for the announcement of the decision in the five combined public school segregation cases.

May 17, 1954— In a landmark decision, the Supreme Court of the United States announced that the "separate but equal" doctrine used to establish segregation in public schools was unconstitutional, even when the separate schools were found to be equal based on "objective" factors.

The Court ruled unanimously that intangible issues foster and maintain inequality because racial segregation in public education has a detrimental effect on minority children in that it is interpreted as a sign of inferiority. "Separate but equal" is inherently unequal in the context of public education. Thus the segregation laws violated the equal protection provisions of the Fourteenth Amendment and were unconstitutional.

The case was referred to as *Brown v. Board of Education of Topeka*, but, as noted, it actually was combined with other similar cases. However, on the same day the Court issued a separate ruling that segregation in the District of Columbia was unconstitutional because it violated the due process clause of the Fifth Amendment. This was because the Fourteenth Amendment did not apply to the District of Columbia.

The Court realized the far-reaching impacts of its decision, and it scheduled arguments for October 1954 to determine the remedy for the unconstitutional behavior. But these arguments would be further delayed until April 1955. Thus the present decision would be known as "Brown I" while the decision in 1955 on how to implement Brown I would become known as "Brown II."

The District of Columbia and some border states began immediately to desegregate their schools. By fall, 150 school districts in eight states had been integrated. But state legislatures in Alabama, Georgia, Mississippi, South Carolina, and Virginia adopted resolutions of "interpolation and nullification" that declared the Court's decision to be null, void, and of no effect. Various southern legislatures passed laws that imposed sanctions on anyone who implemented desegregation, and they also enacted school closing plans that authorized the suspension of public education, and the disbursement of public funds to parents to send their children to private schools. The battle lines were clearly drawn.

May 22, 1954— On this date the school board of Little Rock, Arkansas, issued a policy statement saying it would comply with the United States Supreme Court decision on desegregation that was issued the previous week when the Court outlined the method to be followed and the time to be allowed.

This was a significant step in the upcoming integration battle. Little Rock would become a symbol throughout the world of the difficulties of public school integration following the Supreme Court decision in Brown I and Brown II. The school of law at the University of Arkansas had been integrated in September 1949, and the Little Rock Public Library had been integrated in January 1951. But the election of Orval E. Faubus as governor of Arkansas in the fall of 1954 changed the atmosphere. Faubus was a dedicated segregationist.

October, 1954— Justice Robert Jackson of the United States Supreme Court died suddenly during this month and John Marshall Harlan was nominated as a replacement by President Eisenhower. Harlan was, ironically, the grandson of the lone dissenter to the Plessy decision of 1896 that established the "separate but equal" doctrine, which the *Brown* decision had just overthrown. After a long hearing before the Senate, Harlan was sworn in as an associate justice in March 1955.

April 1955— During this month, the United States Supreme Court heard its third round of arguments on public school segregation. This time the hearings concerned the remedies to be applied to the case.

May 24, 1955— The school board of Little Rock, Arkansas, voted unanimously to adopt the plan of Superintendent Virgil Blossom to gradually integrate the schools starting in September 1957. The plan would start at the high school level and add the lower grades over the next six years. Mr. Blossom was named "Man of the Year" by the *Arkansas Democrat* for his work on desegregation.

May 31, 1955— The Supreme Court of the United States issued the directives to help implement its decision of May 17, 1954, (see entry) essentially forbidding racial discrimination in public schools. The Court found that the problems identified in its decision the previous year ("Brown I") required varied local solutions. Local school districts and the courts which originally heard school segregation cases were to work together to implement the principles of Brown I "with all deliberate speed."

This decision would be known as "Brown II" and would be roundly criticized by many experts in the future for the vagueness of its "all deliberate speed" phrasing. As could be expected, some states considered a plan that would require decades to phase out segregation to meet the "all deliberate speed" requirement. In many ways, the obstacles some states put in the way of desegregation essentially caused the student protests that launched the civil rights movement.

February 3, 1956— Autherine Lucy, a 26-year-old black woman with a college degree from all-black Miles College in Alabama, enrolled as a graduate student in library science at the University of Alabama. Court action to get her into the all-white University of Alabama had begun in 1953, and a court order restraining the university from barring her based on race had been obtained on her behalf by the National Association for the Advancement of Colored People (NAACP) on June 29, 1955.

On the third day of classes in February 1956, mobs of students, townspeople, and out-of-state groups called for her to be killed, threw eggs, and blocked her way until a police escort was needed to get her into class. That evening Lucy was suspended by the university for "her safety" and that of other students. The NAACP filed suit claiming contempt of the court order and claiming the school was acting in support of the mob. They were unable to support these claims, and were forced to withdraw them. The NAACP suit filed on her behalf was then used as justification for expelling Lucy from school.

In an interesting footnote, Lucy returned to the University in 1989 and graduated (together with her daughter) in 1992 (see listing).

February 8, 1956— The National Association for the Advancement of Colored People (NAACP) filed a suit on behalf of 33 black children who had attempted to register in all-white schools in Little Rock since the beginning of the year and were turned down. The NAACP claimed the school desegregation plan proposed previously by the Little Rock school district was too slow and did not meet the definition of "all deliberate speed."

August 28, 1956— Federal Judge John E. Miller dismissed the suit filed by the NAACP in February. Miller ruled that the Little Rock school board had acted in "utmost good faith" in its integration plan (which was to begin in the fall of 1957 at the high school level). The NAACP appealed the decision.

A few weeks later the Little Rock public bus system was quietly integrated.

November 1956— Arkansas Governor Orval E. Faubus was elected to a second term. He was determined to avoid integration in any way possible.

1957— During this year, the number of students taking the SAT annually passed half a million.

April 29, 1957— The Eighth Circuit Court of Appeals in St. Louis upheld the lower court's ruling in August 1956 that the Little Rock school district integration plan was adequate. This permitted the planned integration for September 1957 to go ahead.

During this spring a group of 17 blacks were selected to attend Central High School in the fall, but eight later decided to remain at an all-black school. This left nine to attend the previously all-white Central High School. They would become famous as the "Little Rock Nine."

August 27, 1957— With integration scheduled to begin in September, a member of the Mothers' League of Central High School (a group that was formed over the summer together with the Capital Citizens Council to oppose the integration plan) filed a motion seeking a temporary injunction against school integration. Pulaski County Chancellor Murray Reed granted the injunction on the grounds that "integration could lead to violence."

Federal District Court Judge Ronald Davies nullified the injunction two days later.

September 2, 1957— Arkansas Governor Orval Faubus called out the Arkansas National Guard to "preserve the peace" because he claimed extremists were coming to Little Rock "in caravans." The Guard surrounded Central High School and turned away the nine blacks who attempted to enter Central on September 4 after District Court Judge Davies ordered on September 3 that integration should start the next day.

September 20, 1957— District Court Judge Davies ruled that Governor Faubus was using the National Guard to prevent integration rather than to preserve the peace, as Faubus had claimed. The governor removed the National Guard and the Little Rock Police Department took over.

September 23, 1957— The "Little Rock Nine" black students entered Central High School through a side door and were taken to the principal's office (by a white student), where they received their class assignments. About

1,000 people were milling around in front of the school, and when word was received that the black students were inside the school, the crowd became an unruly mob. The police feared they could not maintain control and the nine black students were removed from the school via a side door.

September 24, 1957— The mayor of Little Rock, Woodrow Mann, sent a telegram to President Eisenhower asking for federal troops to maintain order and to complete the integration process. The president announced he was sending 1,000 troops of the 101st Airborne Division to Little Rock, and he was also federalizing the 10,000-man Arkansas National Guard.

September 25, 1957— The nine black students were escorted to Central High School by the federal troops. The federal troops stayed for two months and then turned the task over to the federalized Arkansas National Guard. Integration continued until graduation in May 1958, but the battle would begin again and run through 1958.

October 8, 1957— The *New York Times* carried an article quoting Dr. Elmer Hutchisson, director of the American Institute of Physics, as saying that the nation's youth must be taught to appreciate the importance of science or the American way of life is "doomed to early extinction."

Hutchisson was referring to the launch of *Sputnik* by the Soviet Union just four days earlier. He said Soviet scientists and teachers had a high place in Soviet society and that Soviet policy, in which science was taken almost as a religion, was obviously paying off.

Hutchisson added that the United States must distinguish between scientific knowledge that can be taught by rigorous discipline and the "namby-pamby" kind of learning that seeks to protect children against inhibition of their individuality, "or their laziness."

It was not the first time the issue of high school curricula had been raised in terms of what high school students should learn and what percentage of high school students should learn it, and it would not be the last time. The issue was raised most vocally when other countries seemed to be moving ahead of the United States, and when the percentage of high school graduates moving on to higher levels of education was deemed to be too low. However, the "shock" of *Sputnik* did result in many more dollars being spent on scientific research and the education processes necessary to support it.

February 20, 1958— The Little Rock School Board filed a request for permission to delay integration until the concept of "all deliberate speed" was defined and until effective legal means existed for integrating the schools without impairing the quality of educational programs.

May 27, 1958— Student Ernest Green became the first black to graduate from Central High School in Little Rock, joining 600 students in commencement ceremonies that were carefully protected by federal troops and city police, and at which no incidents occurred.

June 21, 1958— District Court Judge Harry Lemley granted the delay of integration that was requested by the Little Rock School Board in February of this year. Lemley set a new date of January 1961, stating that blacks have a constitutional right to attend public schools, but "the time has not come for them to enjoy that right." The NAACP immediately appealed.

August 18, 1958— The Eighth Circuit Court of Appeals in St. Louis reversed the District Court judge's ruling of June that integration in Little Rock could be delayed. The Little Rock School Board requested three days later that it be given a 30-day stay to appeal to the United States Supreme Court. The Supreme Court then took only four more days to announce it would hold a special session to discuss the Little Rock school desegregation issue.

While these court actions were taking place, Governor Orval Faubus held a special session of the Arkansas state legislature to pass a law allowing him to close public schools to avoid integration and to lease the closed schools to private school corporations.

September 2, 1958— President Eisenhower signed the National Defense Education Act (NDEA). This act, and the founding of the National Aeronautics and Space Administration (NASA) one month later, was the nation's basic response to the launching of *Sputnik* by the Soviet Union in October 1957. These actions were the gateway to the modern era of federal support for basic research and for stimulating an increase in research and development investments nationwide.

The NDEA was the most important federal act related to education since the Morrill Act of 1862 establishing land-grant colleges and universities. The circumstances of *Sputnik* overcame the basic reluctance of many in Congress to have the federal government take such an active role in education. The legislation stated that "an educational emergency exists and requires action by the federal government. Assistance will come from Washington to help develop as rapidly as possible those skills essential to the national security."

The result was that federal expenditures for education more than doubled. This included funding for student loan programs, graduate fellowships in the sciences and engineering, institutional aid for teacher education, and funding for curriculum development in the sciences, math, and foreign languages. The NDEA provided funding at all levels of education, but its greatest impact was seen in the growth of research universities. It was a true watershed that led to major changes in federal higher education policy. The original act provided $575 million in funds, and additional public laws extended certain specific aspects of the program to the early 1970s.

September 12, 1958— The United States Supreme Court ruled that Little Rock must continue with its integration plan. The school board announced the opening of the city's high schools three days later, but the schools were ordered closed by Governor Faubus. A lawsuit resulted in the state's closing law being found unconstitutional, but this ruling did not occur until June 1959.

September 27, 1958— A special election was held in Little Rock in an attempt to open the schools, but those opposed to integration won by a margin of 17 to 1. The schools were closed for the coming year. About 750 of the 3,698 students enrolled in a newly established all-white private school, while many others left town to live with friends in a place where they could continue their education.

1959— During this year, a new testing organization called American College Testing (ACT) was formed. The new company became the biggest rival to the Educational Testing Service (ETS) (See listing.)

March 1959— During this month the Little Rock Chamber of Commerce voted 819 to 245 in favor of reopening the schools on a controlled minimum integration plan acceptable to the federal courts. The chamber had found the closing of the schools to be bad for business. In the meantime, the school board was in turmoil with its membership evenly divided 3–3 between those favoring compliance to the integration laws and those opposed.

May 25, 1959— A recall election was held in Little Rock, and was narrowly won by a group trying to replace the three segregationist members of the school board (of a total of six members). The segregationist members had tried earlier in the month to fire 44 teachers and administrators suspected of being sympathetic to integration. The three segregationists were replaced by three moderates, making the board consist of a total of six moderates.

June 18, 1959— The Arkansas school closing law was found unconstitutional by a federal court. The newly constituted Little Rock School Board announced that it would reopen the high schools in the fall.

August 12, 1959— The Little Rock School Board opened public high schools a month early. Three black girls quietly attended the new Hall High School in an upper-income area of west Little Rock with no fanfare. Governor Faubus addressed a segregationist rally at the state Capitol, and advised them to make no "rambunctious protest." About 250 people marched to Central High School to make a protest, but the Little Rock police force quickly arrested 21 persons and turned on fire hoses to disperse the rest. Jefferson Thomas and Carlotta Walls, two of the original "Little Rock Nine," returned to Central High for their senior year. All grades of public school in Little Rock would be finally integrated in 1972.

1960— During this year many of the "normal schools" that had begun in California as early as 1857 (later called "teachers' colleges") were combined by the California legislature in a California Master Plan that created an 18-campus statewide California State College system. The campuses in this system were gradually renamed "universities" between 1972 and 1987.

The California State University system became a separate but parallel system to the more prestigious (and more expensive) California University system (see entry for March 23, 1868). The California State University (CSU) system has a common chancellor in charge of the overall system, with each of the 23 campuses having its own president. CSU accepts students who rank within the top third of their high school graduating class, while the University of California system requires that high school students graduate within the top eighth of the class. Many students begin within the CSU system for two years, and then switch to the University system for the final two years to earn a more prestigious degree.

The CSU system has a total of 414,000 students and 44,000 faculty, making it the largest university system in the world. The parallel California University system has 191,000 students with 13,335 faculty. Thus, these two systems alone enroll over 600,000 students in California, with over 27,000 faculty members serving the students. This does not include the over 50,000 students enrolled in the two prestigious private colleges of Stanford and the University of Southern California, or the over 1.6 million students enrolled in 115 California community colleges. In the nation's most populous state, education is a very big business indeed.

1960— During this year the University of California college system began to require applicants to take the SAT. This made the California system the biggest client of the Educational Testing System (ETS). (See listing.)

February 4, 1961— The University of Mississippi denied admission to James Meredith, a black man who was a native of Mississippi. Meredith had served a decade in the Air Force right out of high school, and then attended Jackson State College for two years. Meredith and the NAACP took his case to court in May 1961.

March 6, 1961— For the first time, the words "affirmative action" appeared in an official government document as President Kennedy issued Executive Order 10925, which created the Committee on Equal Employment Opportunity. The order mandated that projects financed with federal funds "take affirmative action" to ensure that hiring and employment practices are free of racial bias.

The emphasis of affirmative action started out in the area of racial bias in hiring practices. However, it soon was expanded to include gender bias and it enveloped all phases of life and became a major issue in admissions to college and in the assembling of teaching staffs everywhere. Today, almost 50 years after its first official use, the phrase "affirmative action" can still be a lightning rod for debate in certain phases of postsecondary education, but its impact has been much reduced in recent decades as both the courts and new state laws have eliminated racial preferences in an effort to achieve a "race-neutral" environment.

September 10, 1962— The United States Supreme Court ruled that the University of Mississippi could not deny admission to James Meredith on the basis of race (see entry for February 4, 1961).

September 25, 1962— The governor of Mississippi, Ross Barnett, blocked the entrance of James Meredith to the University of Mississippi despite a court order to admit him.

September 30, 1962— Riots broke out on the campus of the University of Mississippi and in the town of Oxford, in which the University was located, as James Meredith attempted to attend classes there five days after being denied entrance to the university by Governor Barnett. Over 20,000 United States troops, sent by President Kennedy, did battle with a mob of 3,000 made up of students, local citizens, and the Ku Klux Klan. Before order was restored, two people were killed and 78 United States marshals and soldiers were injured.

Meredith started classes the next day, and graduated on August 18, 1963. He eventually received a law degree from Columbia University in 1968.

June 17, 1963— The United States Supreme Court ruled that a Pennsylvania state law mandating devotional Bible reading in public schools was unconstitutional, even if the law was amended to permit students to opt out, with parental consent, of the religious exercise. The Supreme Court combined the Pennsylvania case (*School District of Abington Township v. Schempp*) with a similar Maryland case (*Murray v. Curlett*) and specified that any such religious exercise with a mandatory component was clearly unconstitutional. The decision was characterized by some analysts as one that "kicked God and prayer out of the schools." However, three decades later a ruling would be made that "student-led and student-initiated" prayer of a "non-sectarian and non-proselytizing" nature would be permitted at graduation ceremonies (see entry for June 7, 1993).

September 24, 1963 — The Health Professions Education Assistance Act was approved. Also known as the "Medical School Bill," the legislation provided $175 million in matching grants for the construction of teaching facilities to train a wide range of medical professionals. Student loans of $61.4 million were also authorized. Subsequent amendments offered further assistance.

The passage of this act and its signing by President Kennedy reflected a growing willingness by Congress to further extend the reach of the federal government into the educational process, and to provide funding for what were considered pressing educational needs.

December 16, 1963 — President Johnson signed the Higher Education Facilities Act of 1963. The purpose of the act was "to authorize assistance to public and other nonprofit institutions of higher education in financing the construction, rehabilitation, or improvement of needed academic and related facilities in undergraduate and graduate institutions." It was another step by the federal government into the process of assisting educational institutions in a financial manner.

August 20, 1964 — President Johnson signed the Economic Opportunity Act (EOA). This act was a key component of what was known as his Great Society and associated War on Poverty campaign (a new presidential election was only a little more than two months away). The EOA was implemented by the later disbanded Office of Economic Opportunity, and it contained several programs to promote the health, education, and general welfare of the poor. Most of these initiatives were subsequently modified, weakened, or completely rolled back by future administrations. However, the Head Start program in education that was created by the EOA became very popular and continues today.

Head Start focuses on assisting low-income children from three to five years of age so they are better prepared to begin school. The program was launched as an eight-week program in the summer of 1965, and then it quickly expanded to a full-year program. It was designed to break the cycle of poverty by providing preschool children with a comprehensive program that addresses their emotional, social, health, nutritional, and psychological needs.

In 1969, the program was transferred to the Office of Child Development in the Department of Health, Education, and Welfare. It now resides in the Department of Health and Human Services, inferring that it is seen as more of a welfare program than an educational program per se. But the program has been a boon to the educational process, getting children who otherwise would have limited resources to apply to the beginning of their school years prepared to begin — and succeed — in their early years of education. The program is generally locally administered by community-based nonprofit organizations that work closely with local school systems.

April 9, 1965 — The Elementary and Secondary Education Act (ESEA) was passed. Part of President Johnson's War on Poverty initiative, the act was essentially based on the concept of redress, i.e., the idea that children from low-income homes required more educational services than children from affluent homes. The act allocated $1 billion a year to schools with a high concentration of low-income children.

President Johnson considered the act the key piece of legislation in his War on Poverty. He forecast that the money spent would come back many times over as "school dropouts change to school graduates" due to their moving out of poverty thanks to the impact of the act. This concept was soon challenged by the Coleman report of 1966, which argued that improvements such as higher quality of teachers and curricula, improved facilities, and even compensatory education had only a modest impact on student achievement.

This legislation signaled a switch from general federal aid to education to categorical aid, and the tying of federal aid to education to national policy concerns such as poverty. It also minimized religious conflict by linking federal aid to educational programs directly benefiting poor children in parochial schools, rather than the schools per se. Finally, relying on state departments of education to administer the federal funds muted criticism of federal control, and resulted in an increase in state government activity in the making of decisions related to education. Many of the specific elements of the act would be changed by future administrations, but the strategies employed in implementing the act would go on into the future.

The act was amended in 1968 to give aid to certain school districts to assist them in implementing bilingual education. This would become another contentious issue in the nation's educational system nearly everywhere it was applied. Many critics pointed out that the practice may help students get better grades in academic subjects taught in their own language, but it ultimately resulted in these students graduating from high school without good proficiency in the English language, the thing they needed most to go on with higher education and/or get good jobs. Bilingual education would essentially disappear in favor of English immersion concepts with the implementation of the No Child Left Behind (NCLB) Act signed early in 2002.

September 24, 1965— For the first time, affirmative action was given the force of law. Executive Order 11,246, issued by President Johnson, required that government contractors take specific measures to insure equality in hiring, and that they must document their affirmative action efforts in order to win the contract. On October 13, 1967, the order was amended to cover discrimination on the basis of gender. It did not take long before affirmative action issues arose in various aspects of education, especially in college admissions.

November 8, 1965— The Higher Education Act of 1965 was passed. This act focused on federal aid to colleges and universities and financial aid to students enrolled in those institutions. It included services to help students complete high school and enter into and succeed in postsecondary education, and the act included aid to improve K-12 teacher training at postsecondary institutions.

November 12, 1968— The United States Supreme Court overturned a ruling by the Arkansas Supreme Court concerning the "anti-evolution" statue of the state. The higher court found that the statue was unconstitutional because it did not forbid teaching all versions of the origin of man, but only those versions in conflict with the Bible. Thus, the higher court reversed the lower court, which had found simply that the state had power to specify the public school curriculum.

1969— In this year both Yale University, since 1701 (see listing) an elite Ivy League school for men, and Vassar College, one of the Seven Sisters and among the elite all-women colleges since 1865 (see listing), became fully coeducational schools.

November 10, 1969— The first broadcast of *Sesame Street* was made on PBS. The educational show became an incredible success, and is presently seen by almost half of all preschoolers in the United States on a weekly basis. It has been broadcast in more than 40 countries and there are at least 10 foreign-language versions.

The show was originally funded by the Head Start program in conjunction with the Carnegie Corporation. It was developed by the Children's

Television Workshop (CTW), which also eventually developed *The Electric Company*. The original urban setting of the show was intended to attract an inner-city audience, but the "Muppets" of Jim Henson proved to be popular among children of all backgrounds. The show teaches preschoolers about letters, numbers, and social values. It represents by far the most successful use of television in the beginning of the educational process.

1970— During this year the prestigious University of Virginia, the school founded by Thomas Jefferson, who saw in his time no role for females in higher education (see listing for March 1825), became a fully coeducational school. Similarly, Johns Hopkins University became fully coeducational in this year as well (see listing for February 1876).

May 4, 1970— Thirteen students at Kent State University in Ohio were shot by members of the Ohio National Guard, and four were killed. The students had been involved in a massive demonstration protesting the invasion of Cambodia, which had been going on since May 1. The university was closed after the shootings, and normal campus activities did not resume until the summer.

This event was the worst in terms of deaths of the many demonstrations that occurred on college campuses during the Vietnam War. Investigations and legal actions following the event went on until January 1979 when a settlement was reached among the 13 victims.

May 25, 1970— The Department of Health, Education, and Welfare (HEW) issued a memorandum that included language more broadly defining the responsibility of school districts to provide bilingual education services to limited-English speakers under the 1968 amendment to the Elementary and Secondary Education Act (ESEA) of April 9, 1965 (see listing).

June 28, 1971— Chief Justice Warren Burger articulated a three-part test for laws dealing with the question of the establishment of religion clause in the First Amendment that come before the Supreme Court of the United States. This test would be used in many futures cases.

The specific case in question was known as *Lemon v. Kurtzman* and dealt with the question of state aid provided to "church-related educational institutions" in Rhode Island and Pennsylvania. Burger stated that "establishment" laws, to be constitutional, must have a "secular legislative purpose," must have principal effects which neither advance nor inhibit religion, and must not foster an "excessive government entanglement with religion."

The Court found that the laws in question, by subsidizing parochial schools, furthered a process of religious inculcation. Also, the continuing state surveillance necessary to enforce the specific provisions of the laws would inevitably entangle the state in religious affairs. Finally, the Court noted that there was "an unhealthy divisive political potential" concerning legislation which appropriates support to religious schools.

The applicable laws were found unconstitutional.

March 1972 — Although some experimental work had been done earlier, during this month Ray Tomilson of BNN, a company that had the contract to build the military ARPANET (a precursor of the Internet), wrote the first fundamental "e-mail" programs. Users originally called e-mail "net notes" or simply "mail." As more computers were added to the ARPANET, e-mail became extremely popular and helped expend the network in an iterative fashion.

No one imagined at the time that as the commercial Internet became established in the 1990s, e-mail via the Internet would become a way for students to complete their college educations without setting foot on a college campus. E-mail would become an important part of the educational process, but it is doubtful if many persons involved in education either as students or teachers took note at the time of the essential birth of e-mail.

May 15, 1972 — The United States Supreme Court found in favor of certain Amish and Mennonite parents in Wisconsin who did not want to send their children to public school until they were 16 years old as required by Wisconsin law. The parents argued that requiring their children to attend school beyond the eighth grade violated their religious beliefs.

The Court held that an individual's interest in the free exercise of religion outweighed the state's interest in compelling school attendance beyond the eighth grade. The Court found that the values and programs of secondary school were "in sharp conflict with the fundamental mode of life mandated by the Amish religion," and that an additional one or two years of high school would not produce the benefits of public education cited by the Wisconsin law.

June 23, 1972 — Amendments to the Higher Education Act of 1965 were approved. The most famous amendment, and the one that had the greatest future impact, was Title IX, which prohibited discrimination in educational opportunities because of sex. Title IX has received its greatest publicity in the area of sports, but it applies to all aspects of education. On October 9, 2002, Title IX was renamed the Patsy T. Mink Equal Opportunity In Education Act in honor of the congresswoman who had worked tirelessly for women's rights in education before her death just the month before.

Recognizing the implications of Title IX, Congress specified that it would not be enacted until 1977, even though the amendment was written in 1972. The act essentially made all institutions of higher education available on an equal basis to both men and women. Thus, the remaining "men only" institutions had to admit women on an equal basis. The five-year gap between writing and enactment gave these institutions time to prepare for the new era. Some still refused until forced to do so when served with a lawsuit they were certain to lose or until faced with an adverse decision from a judge.

A prime effect of Title IX was the rearrangement many schools had to make in the field of sports. Most schools derived the revenue to support all their sports activities from men's football and/or men's basketball programs. Thus, not surprisingly, these programs received the bulk of available sports funds. However, Title IX was interpreted as meaning that schools had to spend roughly an equal amount of funds on sports for both men and women. In many cases this did not result in greatly increased funds for women's sports, but rather a substantial cutback in the number of sports offered to men. The reality was that there were not many other sources of revenue to provide additional funding for women's sports. As a result, schools simply reduced total expenditures to the point where they were divided about equally between the sexes. The men whose sports options were reduced to permit an equal division of funds were understandably upset. This problem continues today and a final resolution is still well into the future.

August 1972—The Economic Opportunity Act was amended in this month to call for expansion of the Head Start program opportunities to handicapped children. The legislation mandated that at least 10 percent of the national enrollment of Head Start consist of handicapped children. By October 1974 there would be over five million children served by the Head Start program.

March 21, 1973—A key issue in school funding was resolved at the national level when the United States Supreme Court announced its decision on a suit brought by the San Antonio, Texas, School District claiming the funding of schools in Texas was unconstitutional because students living in poor areas got fewer funds from property taxes than students living in wealthy areas.

The Court ruled against San Antonio, noting that, first, there is no fundamental right to education in the Constitution, and second, the Texas system (similar to those in most other states) did not systematically discriminate against all poor people in Texas. The Court said that the funding scheme was not "so irrational as to be invidiously discriminatory." Justice Lewis Powell noted that on the question of wealth and education, "the Equal

Protection Clause does not require absolute equity or precisely equal advantages."

The State of California took another route when its supreme court ruled in 1971 and 1976 that its property tax financing system violated the **state** constitution. The court ordered that financing be equalized, with distinctly mixed results. (See "Serrano" entry for 1977.)

June 21, 1973—The United States Supreme Court announced its decision on one of the first cases in which segregation in a northern school was considered since the famous desegregation decisions of May 17, 1954, and May 31, 1955 (see entries). The case concerned the Denver, Colorado, school system, which had been partly segregated since 1960. The complaint was that if the system was partly segregated, the entire system had to be considered illegally segregated. A lower court disagreed.

The Supreme Court ruled that if segregation is proven in one part of a school system, it could be considered "prima facie" proof of segregation in the entire system. The system involved then has the burden of proving that it operated without "segregative intent" on a systemwide basis.

January 21, 1974—Justice William O. Douglas of the United States Supreme Court delivered a unanimous opinion in *Lau v. Nichols* that some felt opened a new era in federal civil rights enforcement under the so-called "Lau Remedies." The case concerned a group of Chinese students who sued the San Francisco school district for not providing special help in learning English in order for them to succeed at school. The Supreme Court overturned a lower court ruling and stated that not providing such help violated the Civil Rights Act of 1964 even if not the United States Constitution.

This decision was seen as another burden on school districts in the name of providing access to all children present in the United States. But the decision did not demand bilingual education per se. It simply stated that some appropriate special help must be provided for such students. By the 1990s bilingual education had fallen out of favor in many areas. By means of ballot initiatives, the state of California in 1998 and the state of Arizona in 2000 essentially eliminated bilingual education in favor of total immersion in English (see listings). The basis for these actions was that total immersion methods were a better approach to the problem. It was shown that bilingual education often led to high school graduates who were not proficient enough in English to get good jobs or to go on to college.

The bilingual issue was essentially dismissed in 2001 when the reauthorization process of the Elementary and Secondary Education Act (ESEA) of 1965 evolved into the No Child Left Behind (NCLB) Act of 2002. This act gave clear preference to having non-English speaking school children learn English sufficiently well to take further instruction in English, rather than using bilingual approaches.

July 25, 1974— The Supreme Court of the United States issued a critical ruling concerning how far the courts could go in attempting to correct a case of segregated school systems. The case concerned public schools in Detroit, Michigan, which were found to be segregated as a result of official policies. Local courts approved a plan involving outlying school districts in the Metropolitan Detroit area.

The Supreme Court ruled that if there was no significant violation by the outlying school districts, and no evidence of any interdistrict violation or effect, then the proposed plan was "wholly impermissible" and was not justified by the Brown ruling. The Court added that achieving desegregation did not require "any particular racial balance in each school, grade, or classroom." The Court also emphasized the importance of recognizing local control over the operation of schools.

1975— The Education of all Handicapped Children Act (EAHCA) was passed this year. It mandated a free appropriate public education (FAPE) for all children with disabilities. This imposed a new burden on schools in terms of the funds needed to make school facilities capable of accepting handicapped children, and to prepare teachers who could deal with such children in the classroom (the majority of the handicaps are mental or emotional). It was another step in the process of making schools accessible to everyone in the population in the United States to an extent far exceeding that offered by any other nation.

The act was known as Public Law 94–142 and was modified several times after 1975. It finally became known as the Individuals with Disabilities Education Act, or IDEA, in 1990 (see listing). As with many such federal government programs, the number of problems defined as a "disability" has steadily increased, and the number of children covered by the act has also steadily increased. Over 6 million children are now covered by the program, including over 200,000 infants and toddlers in preschool programs.

1976— The granting of access to a college education for females, nearly complete by now in the United States, finally reached the military academies this year. The United States Military Academy, the United States Naval Academy, the United States Air Force Academy, and the United States Coast Guard Academy were officially opened to female undergraduates. The United States Merchant Marine Academy had been opened to females in 1974.

Related public all-male military-oriented colleges such as the Citadel and the Virginia Military Institute (VMI) would be opened to females in 1993 and 1997, respectively (see listings).

1977 Serrano— In 1977 the California Legislature took action to reflect rulings in 1971 ("Serrano I") and 1976 ("Serrano II") by the California Supreme Court. The court ruled that the California property tax system for funding schools violated the equal protection clause of the state constitution because students in poor districts got less funding than students in wealthy districts. The United States Supreme Court rejected this issue on a national level (see entry for March 21, 1973), but California decided on a different approach. It started a long chain of events that ended with California, for a variety of reasons, going from near the top in per-pupil funding to near the bottom.

In 1977, the California Legislature passed Assembly Bill 65 (AB65) to conform to the changes ordered by the state supreme court in Serrano I and Serrano II. The bill would equalize revenues by increasing state funds for "poor" communities while capping funds for "wealthy" communities and diverting some of their funds to poorer communities. The funds did become nearly equalized by the late 1990s, but many changes took place in the splitting of funding between state and local communities along the way.

In his book *First to Worst*, by John Mockler, the author noted that "Like many mass interventions, the Serrano decisions had unintended negative consequences greater than any gain ever pursued." Other experts agreed that there were two significant negative consequences. Capping per-pupil revenues in high-spending districts overlooked the fact that 75 percent of poor children lived in high-spending districts such as San Francisco and Oakland. Thus, the Serrano decision actually led to lower school spending for most poor children.

Further, the public reaction tended to focus on the recognition that higher local property taxes did not necessarily result in greater support to local schools, and thus the already high taxes became an anathema. In 1978 there was a great property tax revolt in California, and the people passed Proposition 13 that limited property taxes to 1 percent of the assessed value while limiting increases in the assessed value. This caused a revolution in funding of schools, requiring much more money from the state, which raised most of its money from income taxes. The law of unintended consequences continues to hold everywhere.

June 28, 1978— A decision was handed down by the United States Supreme Court that forbid the use of racial quotas in college admissions policies. The decision was granted in favor of Alan Bakke, who was refused admission to the medical school of the University of California at Davis, even though he had higher qualifications than a number of minority applicants. The school had set aside a quota of 16 percent minority applicants to maintain a "diverse" student body in the interest of affirmative action.

The Court ruled that race could be one, but only one, of several factors used by "discriminatory boards," like those of college admissions. In rulings such as this one, where the Court tries to "split hairs" and give each side some benefit, the ruling fails to resolve the specific issue and ensures that many more such cases will eventually be litigated. The ruling clearly forbids quotas, but it permits "some form" of racial discrimination in the advancement of affirmative action. Almost 30 years later, cases are still being brought to the Supreme Court in an attempt to get a clear picture of how much and what form of discrimination is permissible in meeting the goals of affirmative action.

In this specific case, at least, a clear result was achieved. Bakke was finally admitted to the medical school, and he graduated in 1992.

November 1, 1978 — The Middle Income Student Assistance Act was established. This act modified the provisions for student assistance programs to allow middle-income as well as low-income students attending colleges or other postsecondary institutions to qualify for federal education assistance.

Recessions in 1980 and 1981 caused Congress to choose between continuing the provisions of this act or cutting back on the maximum award under the Pell Grant program. Congress chose to cut the maximum Pell Grant award.

May 4, 1980 — The United States Department of Education was activated. It had been established on October 17, 1979, when President Carter signed the Department of Education Organization Act. This act divided the Department of Health, Education, and Welfare into the Department of Health and Human Services and the Department of Education, which was scheduled to begin operation in May 1980.

The original Department of Education was created in 1867, but it was demoted to an Office of Education in 1868 when many in Congress feared that it would exercise too much control over local schools. The Office of Education primarily collected information and statistics about the nation's schools.

The Department of Education created in 1980 was charged with the task of ensuring access to educational opportunity for every individual and of promoting excellence in the nation's schools. To achieve these goals, the department administers and coordinates federal assistance programs for education. The department now has about 4,500 employees and a budget of over $60 billion. But as explained in the introduction, achieving equal access to schools for everyone and also achieving a high degree of excellence in the schools are nearly mutually exclusive goals. Controversies and litigation go on continually among groups that want to emphasize one goal over the other. The nation is very close to achieving equal access for everyone, but it is far from achieving a standard degree of excellence, or even reaching agreement on what constitutes excellence in education.

1982— During this year, the Mississippi University for Women was sued by a man seeking admission to the school's nursing program. The case went to the United States Supreme Court, and the university was ordered to admit men. The Court found that excluding men not only violated the equal protection clause of the Fourteenth Amendment, but it was not beneficial to women because the policy furthered the image of nursing as "women's work."

1982— The Perkins School for the Blind (see entry for 1829) changed its charter during this year to admit students with multiple handicaps other than blindness. Perkins had become known throughout the world for providing services to blind and deaf and blind students, and it was decided the resources that had been developed at the school in the last 150 years could help greatly in educating persons with multiple disabilities of many types.

June 15, 1982— In a decision that continues to produce a severe financial impact on states with large numbers of illegal aliens, the United States Supreme Court ruled that a Texas law permitting the withholding of state funds for the education of illegal aliens was an unconstitutional violation of the equal protection clause of the Fourteenth Amendment.

The Court ruled that although illegal aliens are not citizens, they are "people" and thus are afforded Fourteenth Amendment protections. Their children are severely disadvantaged by the lack of an education, and since Texas could not show that its regulation served a "compelling state interest," the Texas law was struck down.

June 25, 1982— In a free-speech test, the United States Supreme Court ruled that the removal of certain books from school libraries of the Island Trees Union Free School District was unconstitutional. The school district held that the books were "anti–American, and anti–Christian, anti–Semitic, and just plain filthy."

The Court ruled, in a narrow 5–4 decision, that although school boards have a vested interest in promoting respect for social, moral, and political community values, their discretionary power is secondary to the imperatives of the First Amendment. School libraries are a center for the dissemination of information and ideas, and as such they have "a special affinity with the rights of free speech and press." Thus, the school board could not restrict the availability of books in its libraries simply because its members disagreed with their content.

April 26, 1983 — The National Commission on Excellence in Education issued a report titled *A Nation at Risk*. The report raised an alarm about concerns that the nation's high school students were falling behind other nations in terms of academic performance, and this situation put the nation at risk in terms of being able to compete in the international marketplace. The report had taken 18 months to complete after Terence Bell, the secretary of education for President Reagan, had assembled his panel of experts in August 1981 and gave them the task.

In international comparisons, the report showed that American students never were first or second and often were last when ranked against other industrial nations on 19 academic tests. About 13 percent of the nation's 17-year-olds (40 percent of minorities) were functionally illiterate. Many other defects were noted in the report, and it was shown that College Boards (SAT scores) declined steadily from 1963 to 1980. Business and military leaders were quoted as saying that high school graduates were so deficient in the basic skills of reading, writing, spelling, and computation that they were forced to spend millions of dollars on remedial training courses just to bring workers and trainees up to a ninth–grade level.

The report caused a furor and many educational reforms were proposed. Critics complained that there were many defects in the report in that many of the comparisons with other nations were not on an apples-to-apples basis. Other analysts noted that with the strong emphasis on making schools accessible to everyone in the United States, the quality of education was bound to suffer. They said that the problem of implementing a high degree of academic excellence while maintaining equality in accessibility was a problem that had yet to be solved, and it was one that might be insolvable. This type of problem is still with us today, and it appears to be as intractable as ever.

February 28, 1984 — In a decision having far-reaching effects in terms of defining when a college was receiving "federal assistance" and must follow certain federal regulations, the United States Supreme Court ruled that government financial support via student loans and grants to students of the college meant the college could be classified as "receiving federal assistance."

The college at issue was Grove City College, a small liberal arts school named after the small Pennsylvania city in which it was located. The college studiously avoided any state or federal assistance to remain free of federal or state "red tape." A Title IX lawsuit was brought against the school under the requirements of the education amendments of 1972 (see entry for June 23, 1972). The Department of Education (DOE) concluded that because many students at the school received Basic Educational Opportunity Grants (BEOGs) the entire school could be classified as receiving federal assistance and thus must comply with Title IX.

The Supreme Court agreed with the DOE. However, the Court did add that Grove City, other than in the financial aid department, was free of federal assistance, and thus the college did not have to comply with Title IX if it wished to end its participation in the grant program. But Congress in 1988 eliminated this exception, specifying that any school defined as receiving federal assistance in any area must apply government regulations to all parts of the school.

March 6, 1984— Governor Lamar Alexander of Tennessee (later education secretary under President George H. W. Bush), signed into law a sweeping education reform plan for Tennessee. This led to the initiation of the Student Teacher Achievement Ratio (STAR) experiment that demonstrated clearly how reduced class size greatly aided academic achievement in school.

Project STAR ran from 1985 through 1989 and showed definite improvements in the Stanford Achievement Test in a variety of schools in Tennessee from kindergarten through third grade when class sizes were reduced. The greatest improvements were shown in inner-city schools, while the highest scores were achieved in rural schools. It was found that the smaller class sizes had to be maintained for at least three years for the improvements to be sustained through later grades. The definition of a small class size was 20 students or fewer. The improvements appeared to be especially significant for minority students.

Many other states (and even some foreign countries) have used the STAR results as a basis to attempt to reduce class sizes, especially in kindergarten through grade three. A nonprofit company named HEROS Inc. provides information and results from the basic STAR database.

October 1984— The Head Start program budget exceeded the $1 billion mark during this month and the number of children served since the program began in 1965 reached over nine million.

January 1985— The Carnegie Foundation for the Advancement of Teachers (see entry for November 15, 1905) issued data this month that it said amounted to "an indictment of the schools" in the nation. It confirmed the *A Nation at Risk* report of April 26, 1983 (see listing). Nearly 75 percent of major U.S. corporations surveyed said they had to train new employees in skills they should have mastered in high school. More than $40 billion was being spent annually to train workers, including remedial education.

The Committee for Economic Development issued a similar report later in the year. During the decade of the 1980s, a majority of states bolstered their graduation requirements, including stronger math and science requirements.

June 4, 1985 — In another test of the First Amendment clause forbidding the establishment of any religion by the government (the establishment clause), the United States Supreme Court announced that an Alabama law authorizing teachers to conduct regular religious prayer services and other activities in classrooms during the day was unconstitutional.

May 19, 1986 — The United States Supreme Court ruled that the action of the Jackson, Michigan, Board of Education in protecting minority employees in the name of affirmative action by first laying off nonminority teachers with more seniority was not constitutional. The Court ruled that injuries to innocent persons due to preferences in hiring are diffused to a considerable extent among society generally. However, injuries to innocent persons due to preferences in layoffs are much more severe. Denial of a possible future employment opportunity is not as intrusive as the loss of an existing job.

October 8, 1986 — Public Law 99–457 extending educational benefits to handicapped children who were preschoolers aged three through five was signed by President Reagan. This was an amendment to the Education for the Handicapped Act passed in 1975 (see listing). The new law also made provisions to help states develop early intervention programs for infants and toddlers with disabilities.

June 19, 1987 — In yet another case dealing with the teaching of evolution, the United States Supreme Court found unconstitutional a Louisiana law entitled Balanced Treatment for Creation-Science and Evolution-Science in Public School Instruction Act. This law held that evolution could not be taught in the schools unless accompanied by "creation science" based on biblical beliefs.

The Supreme Court held that the primary effect of the Louisiana law was to advance the viewpoint that a supernatural being created humankind, and the promotion of this viewpoint was clearly unconstitutional.

September 1989 — During this month, President George H. W. Bush convened the 50 governors of the United States in Charlottesville, Virginia, to discuss education at the first-ever National Educational Summit. They agreed on six national goals (which later grew to eight), including one which would have American students rank first in international tests on math and science by the year 2000. Although this action gave impetus to more standardized testing in schools, the nation's huge and growing diversity in both local school boards and students made the goals difficult to achieve.

April 18, 1990 — In a complicated case again addressing how far courts could go to accomplish the task of eliminating segregation in schools, the United States Supreme Court announced a mixed decision in a case concerning the Kansas City, Missouri, School District (KCMSD). The Kansas City district wanted to try to attract white students from the suburbs by enhancing the quality of its schools. A District Court judge ordered an increase in local property taxes to raise the necessary funds. Opponents claimed he lacked the authority to do so.

The Supreme Court ruled the lower court had indeed "abused its discretion" by imposing a specific tax, but the Court also held that funds could be raised in a different manner because the courts had power to require the state to raise such funds when a "constitutional justification" existed. Otherwise, local governments could fail to fulfill the requirements that the Constitution imposes on them.

May 1990 — During this month Tim Berners-Lee, an English computer analyst working at the CERN Laboratories in Switzerland, resubmitted a proposal for building an information retrieval system to use in his work there. He had submitted a similar proposal in 1989, and when the new proposal was shelved in the same manner as the previous one had been, Berners-Lee essentially decided to take action on his own.

The name Berners-Lee chose for his project was "The World Wide Web," a name he believed would reflect the global nature of his planned network, a network that would be ever growing without end. His persistence in convincing others to try the system led to what we now know as the Internet. The Internet developed into a new way of doing business around the world, and it became a revolution in the educational process.

The Internet is a new source of reference material that is constantly updated and made available to schools at all levels. Also, in conjunction with e-mail (see entry for March 1972) the Internet makes it possible for college students to complete their education without ever setting foot on campus. Some analysts have claimed that the old college system in the United States is outdated. No longer will expensive buildings of bricks and mortar be needed to accommodate students. They can "attend" college from anywhere in the nation without leaving home. The entire concept of a "college education" will change, with great savings in the cost of achieving a degree. Many decades from now, students and educators will look back in wonder at the inefficiencies of the old system.

July 1990— President George H. W. Bush and the nation's governors formed the National Educational Goals Panel to follow up on their National Education Summit in September 1989 (see listing). The following years saw the supporting proposals for these goals come to be called "America 2000." One of the governors deeply involved in the program was Bill Clinton of Arkansas. After he became president in 1992, he built on the program and named it "Goals 2000." He later signed a bill identified as Goals 2000: Educate America Act (see entry for March 31, 1994).

October 30, 1990— The Education for All Handicapped Children Act that was passed in 1975 (see listing) and amended in October 1986 (see listing) was amended again and signed by President Bush. The new version was designated as Public Law 101–476, and among other things the name of the law was changed to the Individuals with Disabilities Education Act or IDEA. It has been known by that name ever since.

December 6, 1990— In a demonstration of how many people think education is an answer to a wide number of social ills, the *Los Angeles Times* of this date carried an article titled "Lobbyists Greet Class in Ethics with Yawns." The essence of the article was that an unusually strong wave of corruption in the state legislature resulted in the legislators passing a law requiring lobbyists to attend a class on ethics.

1991— The first charter school act was passed by the state of Minnesota during this year. By the end of the decade 36 other states had followed the lead of Minnesota. Charter schools were publicly funded but had less strict regulatory requirements than normal public schools in the hope that the teachers in such schools could concentrate more on the students and thus achieve better educational results, especially among minority students.

April 28, 1991— An advertisement appeared in the *New York Times Magazine* of this date that was signed by John Akers, chairman of the world-famous IBM Corporation. The ad stated that education is a "major economic issue." It added that "in an age when a knowledgeable work force is a nation's most important resource, American students rank last internationally in calculus and next to last in algebra." The ad was another salvo in the argument about what subjects students should be taught in the nation's schools.

October 7, 1991— A bill was introduced to amend the Individuals with Disabilities Education Act (IDEA) that was established in October 1990 (see listing) to include all previous acts in this area. The new amendments became Public Law 102–119. They primarily expanded the definitions of childhood problems that could be classified as "children with disabilities" so they could receive benefits under the act.

Spring 1992— Autherine Lucy Foster, who had been enrolled at the University of Alabama as a graduate student in February 1956 (see listing) but was later forced to leave due to subsequent riots, graduated with a master's degree from the university. She was accompanied by her daughter, Grazia, who earned a degree at the same time.

Lucy had been encouraged to re-enroll at the university by several faculty members who heard reports of a speech she was invited to give at the university by two professors about her prior experiences. The faculty members got the university to overturn her expulsion of over three decades ago. At the age of 63, Autherine Lucy Foster got the degree she had attempted to get when she was just Autherine Lucy at the age of 26.

June 24, 1992— The United States Supreme Court ruled in a 5–4 decision that prayers delivered at graduation ceremonies by a religious authority that was "instructed" by school authorities was unconstitutional (*Lee v. Weisman*). The decision added that the fact students could "voluntarily" opt out of the ceremonies was specious because the cultural pressures on teenage students to conform make the word "voluntarily" meaningless. The Court made it clear that any apparent involvement of the authority of the school system in any apparent religious exercise of any nature was unconstitutional.

July 23, 1992— President Bush signed the Higher Education Amendments of 1992. These amendments reauthorized the many programs in the Higher Education Act of 1965, which must be reauthorized every five years to continue in force. This provides an opportunity to add amendments, provide for growth, and make changes.

President Bush did propose changes, primarily focusing on academic achievement. He proposed "Presidential Access Scholarships," and some first steps of what he called his AMERICA 2000 strategy directed at alternative teacher certification programs. The core of the program continued to be financial support for students, but newer elements were also being considered each time reauthorizing amendments were processed.

June 1, 1993— The United States Supreme Court declined to review a court case challenging the language of the Pledge of Allegiance, which is recited daily in most schools in the nation. The challenge was based on the claim that the words "under God" in the pledge violate the separation between church and state specified in the Constitution. In refusing to hear the case, the Supreme Court let stand a lower court ruling permitting the language. The assumption was that the Supreme Court considered that the phrase "under God" had become "secularized" and was not a violation. But the lower court ruling applied only to the Fifth Circuit (Texas, Louisiana, and Mississippi) where the case was brought. It was correctly anticipated that this issue would arise again in the future.

June 7, 1993— The United States Supreme Court declined to hear a case regarding prayer in public schools. The lower court had ruled in *Jones v. Clear Creek Independent School District* that students can vote for a graduation prayer as long as the prayer is approved by the school as nonsectarian and nonproselytizing. The Supreme Court allowed the ruling to stand. This puzzled many analysts who felt the new ruling was in conflict with a prior Supreme Court ruling that even nonsectarian prayers in public schools violate the Constitution. But in this case the students essentially initiated and led the prayer, which was of a nature that was sufficiently "neutral" to pass muster at the lower court.

The Supreme Court's refusal to act delighted the American Center for Law and Justice (ACLJ), which issued a "special bulletin" to every public school district in the United States advising them on how to have prayer included in graduation ceremonies, valedictorian addresses, and baccalaureate services. The American Civil Liberties Union (ACLU) immediately prepared a press release taking issue with both the ACLJ bulletin and the refusal of the Supreme Court to hear the case. The lines were drawn for this issue to appear in the courts again. The refusal of the Supreme Court to make a ruling meant that the decision in this case was valid only in the Fifth Circuit where the lower court had made the ruling that was unsuccessfully appealed to the Supreme Court.

An additional ruling on this date also gave a victory to a group claiming violation of its free speech rights by a school district enforcing a statue against the use of school property after school hours by a religious group. Lamb's Chapel wanted to use the facilities of the Center Moriches School in New York to show religious and family-oriented films after school hours. A state law prohibited use of school facilities, even after hours, by any religious group.

The justices ruled unanimously in favor of Lamb's Chapel. First, they pointed out that the state law prohibited use of school facilities only by religious groups. The establishment clause requires that use of public facilities in such cases be "viewpoint neutral," not opposed only to religious views.

Second, permission to use the facilities would not amount to an establishment of religion because the showings would be neither school-sponsored nor closed to the public.

This ruling emphasized again that the Constitution prohibits both the government-sponsored promotion of a religion as well as the demotion, so to speak, of a religion. Public schools must take both sides into account in their dealing with religious issues.

June 18, 1993— In an increase in the complexities of applying the establishment clause of the First Amendment, the Supreme Court of the United States announced that it was constitutional for parents to request an interpreter be supplied by a Catholic school for a child who had been deaf since birth. The parents requested relief under the provisions of the Individuals with Disabilities Education Act (IDEA). A lower court ruled that public funds could not be used for the interpreter because the interpreter would be a conduit for the student's religious inculcation and so using public funds for the interpreter would be in violation of the First Amendment.

The High Court ruled in a 5–4 opinion that IDEA provides help to handicapped children and it is the private decision of the parents as to what school the aid should apply to. IDEA is "neutral" in this issue, the Court said, and thus the state has nothing to do with the choice and therefore is not promoting a specific religion when the aid is provided.

March 31, 1994— The Goals 2000: Educate America Act of 1994 was signed by President Clinton (see entry for July 1990). The act provided resources to states and communities to ensure that all students "reach their full potential" based on the premise that students will reach higher levels of achievement when more is expected of them. The budget bill of 1996 signed on April 26, 1996, amended the Goals 2000 Act in several important ways, most of which had to do with providing more flexibility in meeting the goals of the act. However, the original Goals 2000 Act mandated the creation of the National Education Standards and Improvement Council (NESIC), which had the authority to approve or reject standards established by the states. This concept was strongly opposed as a national school board by the Republicans, who gained control of Congress in the fall of 1994. They felt it was too much of an increased federal role in the educational system, and no one was ever appointed to serve on the council.

June 12, 1995— In an important affirmative action ruling, the Supreme Court of the United States ruled that extreme scrutiny must be applied to affirmative action programs to be sure rules favoring "socially and economically disadvantaged individuals" are not based solely on racial classifications.

The specific case (*Adarand Contractors v. Pena*) concerned subcontracting on a highway project, but the concept of the ruling applies equally well to affirmative-action issues that often arise in education. The court added that race is not a sufficient condition for a presumption of disadvantage, and that proof of past injury does not in itself establish the suffering of present or future injury.

June 26, 1995—In a ruling that upheld the right of schools to conduct random drug tests as a condition of student participation in athletics, the United States Supreme Court ruled that such tests were promoting a legitimate government interest in the safety of minors under their supervision and this outweighed the basic minimal, if any, intrusion into student privacy.

The case involved the Veronia School District in Oregon. The school district heard rumors that athletes were involved in illegal drug use, and on the basis that this increased the risk of sports-related injury, the district instituted random drug testing. When objections were raised by parents about giving consent to such tests before their children could participate in sports, the issue arrived at the Supreme Court.

The Court ruled that testing was a "reasonable" action of the school district, which was responsible for the athletes during school hours, that the collection of the urine samples were in conditions similar to the use of public restrooms, and that the results were viewed only by limited authorities. This was a case where the responsibilities of the school district for minors in their care outweighed personal privacy concerns.

July 19, 1995—President Clinton noted in a speech on this date that although the United States Supreme Court recently had ruled (in a case concerning subcontracting; see entry for June 12, 1995) that affirmative action must be given "strict scrutiny" to avoid abuses in its name, it still was a necessary process. In a White House memorandum issued the same day, President Clinton called for the elimination of any affirmative-action program that creates a quota, creates preferences for unqualified individuals, creates reverse discrimination, or continues even after its equal opportunity purposes have been achieved.

July 20, 1995—The Board of Regents of the University of California voted to end race-based preferences in admissions, hiring, and contracting. The ban would go into effect in 1996 at graduate and professional schools, and in 1998 in the undergraduate division.

1996—Net Day was held during this year to kick off a national effort to wire as many schools as possible to the Internet (see entry for May 1990).

March 1996— The second National Education Summit convened during this month, but the second summit was much different than the first (see entry for September 1989). The first summit was run by President George Bush with the nation's 50 governors in attendance. Many of the goals of that summit got entangled in Washington, D.C., politics, even though President Clinton tried to continue the work started by President Bush.

The second summit was organized by a number of corporate CEOs led by Louis Gerstner, CEO of IBM, and a group of the 50 governors of the United States. President Clinton was only an invited guest. The emphasis of the summit was on removing responsibility for the achievement of education goals from Washington and turning it over to the governors of the states, in conjunction with a number of CEOs from businesses in the various states. A key goal was setting academic standards at state and local levels.

An organization called Achieve Inc. was established after the summit to follow the setting of academic standards. A later opinion poll found that 75 percent of respondents thought that school standards were set too low. But a conflict continued over the issue of how much the federal government should be involved in setting academic standards.

March 18, 1996— In a ruling that set new limitations on affirmative action, the Supreme Court let stand a ruling by the United States Court of Appeals for the Fifth Circuit that became known as the Hopwood ruling. Cheryl Hopwood and three other white students sued the University of Texas law school because they were rejected in favor of less qualified minority applicants.

The result was that the court of appeals suspended the admissions program at the university and in essence overturned part of the Bakke decision from 1978 (see listing). The Bakke decision rejected the use of quotas, but stated race could be a factor in admissions in the interest of maintaining a "diverse" student body. The Hopwood decision, however, asserted that "educational diversity is not recognized as a compelling state interest." The attorney general for the State of Texas later announced in 1997 that all Texas public universities should employ race-neutral admission criteria.

To demonstrate how difficult it is to keep college admission policies compliant with affirmative-action policies, this ruling was itself overturned on June 23, 2003 (see listing).

June 26, 1996— In a ruling that had broad ramifications, the United States Supreme Court ruled against the Virginia Military Institute (VMI) and its long-standing tradition of admitting only male underclassmen.

It was a complicated case. A District Court ruled in favor of VMI, only to be overturned by the Fourth Circuit Court of Appeals. VMI then proposed to create a Virginia Women's Institute for Leadership (VWIL) as a parallel program for women — essentially another "separate but equal" solution. The District Court and the Fourth Circuit Court of Appeals found this solution acceptable; the court of appeals ruled that the two programs offered "substantively comparable" educational benefits.

But the Supreme Court held that in today's world, gender-based classifications must be evaluated with "heightened scrutiny," and that under that standard VMI's plan was unacceptable. The Court tried to emphasize that the times would no longer accept gender-based educational or other classifications except in very extraordinary circumstances.

In light of the firm ruling of the Court, VMI decided to become a coeducational public school rather than the private institution it would have to become to avoid the admission of women. The Citadel of South Carolina had already done so in 1993. This ended the long history of all-male public military institutions in the United States. As is often the case, the economic costs of becoming a private institution to avoid the regulations required of public institutions outweigh even the most deeply held philosophical beliefs. The United States military also became coeducational in its various officer-training establishments in this year. An era truly had ended.

November 5, 1996 — On this date Proposition 209, which banned all forms of affirmative action, was passed by public vote in California. The ban, which would spend almost a year in court before becoming effective, was very basic. It read simply that "The state shall not discriminate against, or grant preferential treatment to, any individual or group on the basis of race, sex, color, ethnicity, or national origin in the operation of public employment, public education, or public contracting."

March 1997 — In an interview published in *Forbes* magazine, writer Peter Drucker, who is famous for his writings on business management and forecasts of future trends in world developments, predicted that in 30 years, large university campuses will be relics. This will be due both to their high costs, and to the ability to deliver more lectures and classes off campus by satellite or two-way video at a fraction of the cost. Today's buildings are hopelessly outdated and totally unnecessary.

The growing tendency for students to pursue their degrees via e-mail over the Internet would tend to support Drucker's analysis.

June 4, 1997 — The newest amendments to the Individuals with Disabilities Education Act (IDEA) restructured IDEA (see entries for October 1990 and October 1991) into four basic parts: General Provisions; Assistance for All Children with Disabilities; Assistance for Infants and Toddlers with

Disabilities; and National Activities to Improve the Education of all Children with Disabilities. The amendments became Public Law 105–17.

June 23, 1997— In an example of the difficulties involved in maintaining state and local laws to be sure they are constitutional, especially in First Amendment cases regarding the establishment clause, the United States Supreme Court announced that it was reversing a decision made in 1985 (*Aguilar v. Felton*) concerning the use of public funds from Title I of the Elementary and Secondary Education Act of 1965 to pay salaries of state employees who teach in parochial schools.

In 1985, the Court held that this was not permitted, essentially because it would lead to the "intrusion" of church and state on each others' respective domain in violation of the "intent" of the establishment clause. In 1997, the Court ruled that there was no evidence the problems they anticipated had actually taken place, and the careful way in which the funds were applied did not violate the establishment clause. Further, the Court said that from now on only those policies which generate an "excessive" conflict between church and state will be deemed to violate the First Amendment.

August 3, 1998— Proposition 227, which essentially banned bilingual education except under certain circumstances, took effect in California. This proposition was passed earlier by voters and withstood a court challenge before it could be implemented in the public schools of the state. Proposition 227 directed the use of English immersion programs to help limited-English speakers become proficient in English, rather than the use of bilingual programs which had been in general use in the United States since the creation of the Title VII amendment to the Elementary and Secondary Education Act (ESEA) in 1965 (see listing. Title VII was added to ESEA in 1968, as noted in the 1965 listing).

Actually, the mandate in the United States has been that public schools are obligated to provide special help for limited English speakers, rather than letting them "sink or swim." The "special help" did not have to be bilingual education per se (see listing for January 21, 1974) but it usually took that form. However, many critics pointed out that bilingual education too often resulted in high school graduates with poor proficiency in English, the one thing they needed more than any other. The result was Proposition 227 in California and the closely related Proposition 203 in Arizona (see listing for November 7, 2000).

October 7, 1998— President Clinton signed the ninth "five-year" reauthorization of the Higher Education Act. Originally passed in 1965 under President Johnson, the act must be reauthorized at least every five years to remain in force. This provides opportunities to modify the act as conditions change.

The core of the act is providing federal support to students attending colleges and universities. This includes Pell Grants, various student loan programs, and the Federal Family Educational Loan Program (FFELP). The next reauthorization is scheduled for 2004–05. Various items relating to academic performance have been added to the act over the years, and more are likely by the next reauthorization.

December 3, 1998 — Voters in Washington State passed a ballot initiative similar to the one passed in California on November 5, 1996 (see listing), that banned all form of affirmative action in the state.

May 20, 1999 — The United States Senate Committee on Health, Education, Labor & Pensions held a hearing to examine the effects of Channel One in the nation's schools. Although there was much testimony by those opposed to the program, no notable action was taken. The controversial Channel One program began in 1990. Channel One provides equipment and programming to the schools that enroll in the program in exchange for providing 12 minutes of news and related subjects to its secondary-school audience of teenagers. The 12 minutes includes two minutes of advertisements directed to the teenagers, who certain advertisers are anxious to reach. The controversy is over whether receiving these ads is a small price to pay for bringing new technology into the classroom and exposing students to current events.

Channel One now reaches about 8 million students in more than 400,000 classrooms in over 12,000 schools across the nation. It is banned by law in the state of New York. It is essentially just another issue in the ongoing argument over what students should be taught in high school and in what manner it should be taught. Since its inception in 1990, Channel One has received more than 150 news and educational programming honors through 2005, including the prestigious George Foster Peabody Award. The Channel One Network supposedly is the largest source of news and public affairs for young people.

2000 — At the beginning of the new millennium, there were over 90,000 public schools in the United States, with 46.5 million students and 2.8 million teachers (about 17 students per teacher). The high school graduation rate for 18-year-olds was 67 percent.

February 22, 2000 — On this date the State of Florida banned race as a factor in college admissions. The ban was made effective when the Florida legislature approved the education component of Governor Jeb Bush's One Florida initiative aimed at ending affirmative action in the state.

June 19, 2000— The United States Supreme Court issued a ruling that a school policy permitting even student-led, student-initiated prayer at football games violated the establishment clause of the First Amendment to the Constitution. This amendment states that Congress "shall make no law respecting an establishment of religion," and so-called "church-state" issues are also often called "establishment clause issues."

The specific case was "*Santa Fe Independent School District v. Jane Doe.*" The parents of two unnamed children (supported by the ACLU) objected to the prayer activities, and the court ruling opposing the case seemed to turn on the fact that the prayers were before a football game rather than as part of a graduation ceremony, a situation which previously had passed muster before the court (see entry for June 7, 1993).

November 7, 2000— Voters in Arizona passed Proposition 203 banning bilingual education in favor of English-immersion instruction in public schools. The proposition was similar to Proposition 227 passed in California two years earlier (see listing for August 3, 1998). As was the case in California, voters felt that the English-immersion approach would be the best way to help limited-English speakers learn to speak English. The previously used bilingual education approach often resulted in high school graduates who were not proficient in English, the one thing they needed above all others.

Further, contrary to popular thought, bilingual education was not a mandate in the United States. The actual mandate was for "special help" to limited-English pupils, not bilingual education per se. But some states mandated bilingual education on their own, even though many critics felt it failed to sufficiently provide English proficiency at graduation. At any rate, the voters in California and Arizona expressed their will to try English Immersion. The No Child Left Behind (NCLB) Act signed in early 2002 also essentially dismissed bilingual education in favor of English immersion.

2001— In the sports season running from 2000–01, a total of 150,916 women and 208,866 men played on college varsity sports teams. This compares with 29,992 women and 170,384 men who played on such teams in 1971–72, the season before Title IX, which banned sex discrimination in any educational institution receiving federal funds, was passed as part of the Education Amendments of 1972.

January 8, 2002— The No Child Left Behind Act of 2001 was signed by President George W. Bush. The act was intended to improve the performance of the nation's primary and secondary schools by increasing the standards of accountability of states, school districts, and schools. It also provides parents more flexibility in choosing which schools their children will attend. The act promoted an increased focus on reading, and reauthorizes the Elementary and Secondary Education Act (ESEA) of 1965 (see listing).

The act was felt to be an example of bipartisan politics because Democratic Senator Edward Kennedy worked closely with Republican President Bush to get the act passed. However, a great deal of controversy has arisen regarding the overall effect of the act and the manner in which it has been implemented. The primary public issue is the use of standardized tests to constantly measure progress and to essentially punish those schools failing to show improvement by permitting parents to choose to select schools other than the ones doing poorly. There has been controversy for decades over the use of standardized tests on the premise that such tests are invariably inherently biased in favor of or against certain groups of students.

A somewhat less public but equally contentious issue is that some groups see the act as a "stealth act" for the eventual privatization of public schools and the federalization of the educational system. These kinds of emotional issues can be harder to resolve than specific problems that are legitimately identified with the requirements and implementation of the act. The No Child Left Behind (NCLB) Act has been reinforced several times as a major action of the Bush administration and controversies continue to arise on both sides of the issue.

June 2002— A United States Supreme Court ruling during this month seemed to boost the case for vouchers in education when the Court found that a voucher program in Cleveland did not violate the constitutional prohibition on government establishment of religion. The Court ruled that the program in question was "entirely neutral with respect to religion" because it permitted the "participation of all schools within the district, religious or nonreligious."

This ruling increased the number of voucher programs in the United States, but many states have so-called "Blaine Amendments" on their books that explicitly bar aid to religious institutions, and these amendments make it difficult to establish voucher programs if they might involve religious schools.

June 2002— During this month, the trustees of the College Board voted to make dramatic changes in the Scholastic Aptitude Test (SAT). The changes would be effective in March 2005. These changes were being made essentially in response to an attack on the SAT made by University of California President Richard Atkinson in early 2001. Atkinson felt that the SAT was distorting the educational process because children as young as 12 were spending much school time learning how to take the test, which was supposed to be a measure of aptitude rather than a measure of test-taking skills.

Atkinson wanted an achievement test on specific college-preparatory subject matter rather than an aptitude test per se. He claimed that prior data showed this type of test was a much better predictor of college performance. The SAT had been replaced in 1993 by tests called SAT I and SAT II, with the first being more like an aptitude test and the latter being more like an achievement test. Atkinson preferred SAT II.

The College Board said the new test proposed for March 2005 would be much more like SAT II. Atkinson said he was "delighted" with the proposal.

June 23, 2003— After lower courts had issued varying rulings, the United States Supreme Court made a split ruling on cases involving affirmative action in admission policies at the University of Michigan. The Court required the undergraduate policy to be changed because it used a formulaic point system that awarded additional points to minorities. Thus, it did not provide the "individualized consideration" of applicants deemed necessary to attain Supreme Court approval on affirmative-action decisions.

However, the Court ruled that the law school graduate admissions policy was acceptable because it used race as only one of many factors in determining acceptance, and that the goal of achieving a "diverse" student body was one in which the state had a "compelling interest" because educational benefits flowed from such a student body.

This ruling reversed the Hopgood ruling of March 18, 1996 (see entry), which held that diversity was not recognized as a "compelling" state interest. The Michigan reversal was by a 5–4 margin, so other reversals can be expected in the future as the makeup of the Court changes. The constitutionality of affirmative action in school admissions will continue to be in the eye of the beholder.

February 2004— The United States Supreme Court drew another line in the sand in the education/religion debate when the Court ruled in favor of the State of Washington in a case where a college student claimed his right to the free exercise of religion was violated by the state's refusal to grant scholarships for the study of theology. The Court ruled the state had the right to deny publicly funded scholarship money to the student.

August 13, 2004— The State of California and the Public Advocates Inc. entered into a settlement of a lawsuit originally brought in May 2000 by the ACLU and various other groups on behalf of 46 students in 18 school districts in California. The suit claimed that California was abdicating its constitutional responsibilities to provide predominately low-income students of color with the bare essentials necessary for learning: adequate books and classroom materials, credentialed teachers, and clean, safe school facilities.

The settlement resulted in Governor Arnold Schwarzenegger (then-Governor Gray Davis had initially fought the lawsuit in 2000) signing an Education Reforms bill in September 2004 that shifted some funding control from the state to local communities to address some of the issues raised in the lawsuit. He also signed specific bills aimed at specific problems cited in the lawsuit. A judge formally finalized the settlement in March 2005. All those present congratulated the students for persisting in the case, even though lawyers hired by Governor Davis to fight the lawsuit had tried hard to discredit them while taking depositions.

September 8, 2004— Even though the No Child Left Behind (NCLB) Act permits parents to transfer their children from poor-performing schools to better schools, a report in the *Los Angeles Times* showed that relatively few eligible students actually transferred. The reasons range from a lack of parental knowledge about their options to a lack of available classrooms to accept those who wish to transfer.

In Los Angeles last year, only 215 students switched out of 204,000 who were eligible. In Chicago the ratio was 1,097 out of 270,000, and in New York it was 6,828 out of 230,000. However, the point was made that a low number switching is not necessarily bad, because it could indicate that the schools in general are improving.

Many parents are reluctant to have their children leave their neighborhood schools to be bused to better schools, even when the better schools have space available. But often better schools are not made available. In Chicago, for example, only 438 seats were reserved for transfers this year, even though 8,000 students have asked to move. Last year, the ratio was 1,097 seats being reserved compared to 18,000 who wished to move. The district holds a lottery for the available spots. Illinois law bars overcrowding of classrooms to meet the need for NCLB transfers.

Similar ratios exist across the country. It will take some time for the NCLB program to be fully understood and embraced, both by parents and school officials, as is true for any new program. The concept of being permitted to leave a "failing" school in your neighborhood for a better school elsewhere is still quite new in the United States.

November 12, 2004— A report in the *Los Angeles Times* stressed that it will be very difficult for schools in the California school system to show constantly improving test scores every year. There are 6,500 public schools in the state, serving a school population of six million students. About 25 percent of those students are classified has having "limited English abilities." The problem is made steadily worse by a growing number of poor immigrant children on the enrollment list. Further, efforts by some officials to toughen standards so as be sure every graduating student can go on to college seem misapplied in schools where half of the students drop out before 12th grade.

This problem demonstrates the dichotomy involved in trying to increase access to high school for everyone while at the same time looking for constantly improving academic test scores. There is no assurance these nearly mutually exclusive goals can be met.

November 17, 2004—President Bush announced he was nominating Margaret Spellings to be the new secretary of education. Ms. Spellings had been chief domestic advisor to Bush, and she replaced Rod Paige as education secretary. Ms. Spellings had advised Bush on education matters since he was governor of Texas, and had worked closely with Democrats in Washington on the No Child Left Behind (NCLB) Act, Bush's prime effort in the education area since he had become president.

Democrats in Congress generally applauded the nomination because they had worked well with Spellings in prior years. This was in contrast to the considerable acrimony that existed between Paige and the National Education Association (NEA), a nominally Democratic group, in 2004 and in previous years.

November 21, 2004—In a report that carried considerable irony, the *Los Angeles Times* reported that Santa Clara University in northern California was attempting to recruit more boys to attend college there. The irony was due to the fact that until 1960 Santa Clara was an all-male university. Now 57 percent of the 4,550 undergraduates there are female.

The 57 percent female number at Santa Clara happens to match the number of bachelor's degrees now awarded to women across the United States. This is due to the fact that women, once barred from many all-male colleges, began attending college at a higher rate than men about a decade ago. This is beginning to concern some colleges, who worry that a "tipping point" will be reached that will turn off potential attendees, both male and female, who want a more diverse environment when they attend college.

Some say the gender gap is mostly limited to lower-income students and minorities, where the females tend to go to college while the males tend to go directly to work or to the military after high school. Others say the gap crosses both racial and social lines. The academic performance of girls at the high school level now generally outstrips that of boys, but engineering, science, and business schools still have a primarily male flavor among their students. However, for the second consecutive year women outnumbered men in medical school applications this year.

The basic fact is that women are making higher grades at the high school level and thus winning the majority of spots in colleges in total. National college enrollment is now 56 percent female in the United States, and 58 percent of women in high school ranked in the top 10 percent of their class compared with 42 percent of males. However, males still outscore females on the college SAT test, and at a high-tech school such as the California Institute of Technology, the student body is 67 percent male. It is clear that women are generally gaining more spots in liberal arts colleges and thus gaining more spots in total. But the old male/female split in favor of males when it comes to highly technical areas has not changed dramatically over the years.

November 24, 2004— It was pointed out in the *Los Angeles Times* that the new omnibus spending bill awaiting the signature of President Bush would freeze Pell Grants and increase college costs for about 1.2 million college students. Pell Grants are the largest federal grant program in the nation, and grants generally are directed at lower-income students (a term now including families earning between $30,000 and $40,000 per year). The cost of a college education continues to climb.

November 29, 2004— *Time* magazine carried an article about the school district of Ann Arbor, the city in which the prestigious University of Michigan is located. Overall, the three main high schools in the city had a combined SAT score of 1,165, 139 points higher than the national average. Eighty-five percent of graduates went on to four-year colleges. Perhaps such good results could be expected in a city where the vast majority of students come from homes with at least one college-educated parent, and where the median family income is $71,292. But in spite of full integration in the city, blacks typically score 100 points lower on the SAT, average a grade of C versus B for whites, and are almost four times as likely to fail a class as are whites.

These differences are typical when comparing blacks in inner-city schools to whites in suburban schools, but are harder to explain when all students are attending the same good schools in the same well-integrated city. Several programs are under way to try to close the gap, but some experts feel it is the result of distinct cultural differences. John Ogbu, an anthropologist at the University of California at Berkeley who has studied similar problems in middle-class Shaker Heights, Ohio, attributes the gap to a black cultural fear of being labeled as "acting white" if they perform well or study too hard in school.

Famous comedian Bill Cosby, who speaks out on such issues as a black man with a doctorate in education, blames negligent parenting for the bulk of the problem. Barack Obama, a black man who has gained much prominence in the black community and who was recently elected to the United States Senate from Illinois, cites the "acting white" mind-set as a key problem. Clearly, the best educational programs that can be devised will have a hard time succeeding if students and parents are not fully behind the concept of doing well educationally, no matter what the color of the family. The general success of Asian students, where students and parents are almost fanatical about doing well in school, certainly confirms this concept.

December 3, 2004— President Bush signed the reauthorized Individuals with Disabilities Education Act (IDEA — see entry for June 4, 1997) into law. Most provisions of the reauthorized act (now named the Individuals with Disabilities Education Improvement Act of 2004) will take effect on July 1, 2005. It is now Public Law 108–446.

December 4, 2004— Senator Robert C. Byrd, a longtime Democratic senator from West Virginia who is a passionate student of the United States Constitution, inserted an amendment into a spending bill that would require all schools through the college level to spend one day a year teaching students about the Constitution. The mandated day would be September 17, the anniversary of the signing of the Constitution in 1787.

The provision would apply to all schools that receive any sort of federal aid, and the manner in which the reception of federal aid has been defined means that it would apply to nearly all schools. The provision seems innocent on its face, and many agree that knowledge of the Constitution would be a good thing. But others worry that the provision could be a precedent-setting step for inserting government control into what schools teach.

Some educators pointed out that education is clearly a province of the states, according to the Tenth Amendment of the very constitution that Senator Byrd wishes to be studied. The stringent legal provisions of the No Child Left Behind (NCLB) Act have already inserted the federal government too far into the educational process, these educators claim, and the Byrd amendment would be another step in that direction.

The issue demonstrates once again that few actions can be taken in the area of education without generating controversy.

December 6, 2004— A new technological tool to help inner-city schools was being promoted by a black ex-NFL player, according to a report in *Time* magazine. Brady Keys, Jr., who set a still-standing team record with a punt return of 90 yards for the Pittsburgh Steelers in 1964, is now selling a computer system to improve communications in inner-city schools.

Keys is involved with a system called Help Involving Parents (HIP) that is being used by 34,000 students and parents in 29 schools throughout New York City. The program enables teachers and parents to form their own communication network via their telephone or the Internet. Parents can get instant feedback on student absenteeism as well as grades. At Walt Whitman Middle School, PTA attendance rose from 5 to 164 after the program was introduced, and 110 of 127 parents who wanted to transfer their children from the school changed their minds. The school was saved, in that sense, and test scores rose 20 percent. It was further proof, if more is needed, that involving parents in their children's schools greatly improves the educational experience and results.

December 8, 2004— The Bill and Melinda Gates Foundation announced that it was expanding its Early College High School Initiative to more than 25 states by allocating nearly another $30 million to the program. The program is aimed at increasing graduation rates, especially among blacks and Latinos. It allows students to complete up to two years of college education during their high school years.

Foundation officials stated they expected to open 170 such schools by the fall of 2008, which would accommodate 65,000 students. The schools are often placed on existing college or university campuses.

December 11, 2004— It was reported in the *Los Angeles Times* that new legislation signed the previous week by President Bush promised improvements in "special education." This is the area of education that has developed since what became the Individuals With Disabilities Education Act (IDEA) was approved in 1975. Today, more than 6.5 million students qualify for special education services under the act. These services include such things as wheelchair ramps and assistance in class in taking notes. But the major growth in such students is among those with emotional problems, mental challenges, and learning disabilities. A prime problem has been the pressure to incorporate such students into regular classrooms where teachers have to deal with the issue of disrupting a class of perhaps 30 "normal" students to try to meet the needs of a single handicapped student.

The revisions in "special ed" will raise the qualification requirements for special ed teachers, and will allow the use of funds to help students not yet in the education pipeline to get extra help to succeed in regular classes (one study showed that many students in special ed were there simply because they had not been adequately taught to read). The revisions will also give schools more freedom to remove disruptive students from classes and limit parents' right to challenge placements of their children.

The overwhelming issue was the question of funding. The legislation commits the federal government to pay 40 percent of special ed costs. But the same promise was made 30 years ago, and only 20 percent of costs were forthcoming over the years. That made schools cut in other areas to meet the mandated costs of special ed. The new legislation will be an empty promise if funding is not delivered as specified.

December 14, 2004— Google, the software giant known for its very successful "search engine" on the Internet, announced on this date that it will spend about $150 million scanning books from leading university libraries into its search engine. This is simply the most recent (and largest) effort of many entities (including the Library of Congress) to make more scholarly books available online. Copyright issues need to be resolved, but by the end of the decade the Internet clearly will be the library to the world. The costs of maintaining such a reference source should also be lower than those of conventional libraries.

December 15, 2004— A federal study released on this date showed what were termed "mixed results" in a pilot study of 150 so-called "charter schools." These schools operate outside some local, state, and union regulations in the hope that being able to focus completely on teaching will enable the charter schools to achieve better results with their typically low-income minority students than regular schools, burdened with more regulatory issues, are able to do.

The federal study showed better results in reading in charter schools than in regular schools, but somewhat poorer results in math. However, when considering only blacks and Latinos, both types of schools achieved similar results. Critics pointed out that the data was flawed in that there was no measure of how long the students had attended the new charter schools. A Harvard study released earlier in the week showed charter school students doing better than their public-school counterparts in both reading and math.

In the last decade, the number of charter schools has grown to more than 3,000, serving more than one million students. Teachers' unions are opposed to such schools because the teachers at charter schools can escape many of the union regulations in force at standard public schools. California alone has 512 charter schools serving 186,000 students, about 3 percent of the state's total of six million public school students. Many analysts think charter schools hold a great deal of promise because they seem to be able to get better results with low-income minority students, exactly the category that does most poorly in regular schools.

December 18, 2004 — The *Los Angeles Times* carried an article describing what may be yet another advantage of charter schools — creating highly qualified teachers. The article focused on High Tech High in San Diego, California. This charter school, in which fewer than half the students are white, sends all of its graduates to college. More than half of these college-bound students are the first in their families to go to college.

But beyond this success story, High Tech High has become the first individual school in California empowered to train and certify its own teachers. The principal of the school hires teachers who have the knowledge and ability to teach their specific subjects, regardless of whether they have prior teaching experience or the all-important credential to do so. The teachers attend courses at the school after hours and on weekends, and after 14 months they are fully credentialed to teach anywhere in California.

This is a relatively low-cost way to train teachers, and it avoids the problem that many would-be teachers face in meeting the requirement that they must teach full time (essentially without pay) for six months to get their credential. Most teachers do this as part of their last term in college, but teachers outside that system find it hard to afford to do this.

Also, teachers emerging from this system are often well-qualified because they had very good knowledge of their subject and were then credentialed, rather than being taught "how to teach" even if their knowledge of their subject was marginal. The hope is that more such programs can be established to help ease California's teacher shortage, and that the teachers will be of higher quality than the "average" teacher in the state.

December 20, 2004 — The issue of the *Los Angeles Times* published on this date carried three articles focusing on issues related to education in California. The first article concerned the difficulty many charter schools were having in locating facilities for their schools. Charter schools represent a new approach to public schools in that they are relieved of some of the regulatory burdens that fall on ordinary public schools so that their teachers can focus on the difficulties of teaching the usually low-income students that charter schools normally attract. The charter school movement is a dozen years old, and a total of 512 such schools are now located in California. This is a small fraction of the over 9,000 public schools in California, but the charter school movement is growing and initial results are promising. However, land and space of any kind is very expensive in California, and this is hindering the growth of charter schools.

Proposition 39, a ballot initiative in a state famous for them, was passed in 2000 to help charter schools obtain facilities, but as often happens in a litigation-happy society such as the one in the United States, much time is spent in courtrooms trying to compel compliance with the measure. Many educators have stated that the lowered regulatory requirements of charter schools will greatly help in educating the lower-income groups targeted by such schools, but the number of schools cannot grow if facilities cannot be found for their use.

December 20, 2004— A second article in the December 20, 2004, issue of the *Times* concerned with education (the first is listed just above) dealt with the issue of affirmative action at the college level. This article was written by Richard H. Sander, a professor of law at UCLA, who had an article on affirmative action forthcoming in the *Stanford Law Review*.

Sander contended that affirmative action by elite schools in admitting blacks who do not meet normal admission standards was actually producing fewer black lawyers in the general population. Using his extensive research, Sander showed that blacks admitted primarily through affirmative action had considerable difficulty in competing with their more-advanced peers, and thus they were only half as likely to stick with academic careers as were blacks at less prestigious colleges (some researchers found the same problem was keeping blacks out of the sciences).

This "mismatch" of blacks with their environments was having an especially serious effect in legal education. Sander states that as the elite schools admit blacks who normally would qualify only for second-tier schools, the second-tier schools lower their standards accordingly to increase their selection of blacks. The result is a cascade of lowered standards that leave 80 to 90 percent of black law students in a mismatch category.

As a result, half of such black students are in the bottom tenth of their class and are 2 1/2 times more likely to drop out of school than whites. The blacks who hang on to graduation are six times more likely than whites to never pass the bar exam (a test that can usually be taken as many times as necessary to get a passing grade). Sander claims that if racial preferences were dropped at the elite schools, more black students would attend second-tier schools and more black students would eventually graduate, as there would be less attrition in the educational process with fewer "mismatch" effects. The result would be more black lawyers than are graduating today.

Sanders concedes that the debate on affirmative action is so polarized that it is difficult to have careful, credible research reviewed in an objective manner. But he states that some changes are badly needed because the attrition effects of the currents system are so devastating that they threaten all of affirmative action's intended benefits.

December 20, 2004— A third article in the *Times* of December 20, 2004, concerned with education (two others are listed immediately above) was written by Goodwin Liu, an assistant professor of law at the University of California at Berkeley. Liu contends that the conclusion of Richard H. Sander regarding affirmative action (as noted above) is wrong. Liu claims that if blacks had much better results at second-tier or lower schools they would communicate this information among themselves and would go to such schools in the first place.

Liu claims that the difficulties black students encounter at elite schools are due to a fear of doing badly and therefore confirming suspicions that the blacks were admitted only as a result of affirmative action. Also, all minority students lack role models and mentors because of a lack of minority faculty members. Finally, discrimination still exists on many campuses in ways both subtle and overt and this further hampers black students.

Liu feels these educational problems should be improved before any consideration is given to modifying affirmative action, which permits many hard-working blacks to overcome the difficulties he and Sander outline and achieve a degree they otherwise would not have had the opportunity to pursue.

December 25, 2004— *The Los Angeles Times* printed some letters it received commenting on the "dueling" affirmative-action articles published on December 20, 2004 (see listings).

One letter from the Regional Director of the United States Commission on Civil Rights urged caution on any change in affirmative action. He noted a change made in affirmative action in contracting efforts via Proposition 209 did not appear to be bringing the anticipated results. Affirmative action in any area is highly complex, and changes should be made only after careful study by proponents on both sides of the issue.

Another letter, from William Kidder of the so-called "Equal Justice Society," was understandably, considering its origin, opposed to Richard H. Sander's conclusions about the negative effects of affirmative action, and the letter referenced a critique by the writer in a forthcoming issue of the *Stanford Law Review*.

A third letter, from a reader, noted that both articles missed the core issue, which is that giving more points on entrance examinations due to skin color is unfairly biased because skin color is something no applicant can control. Students can accept being beat out by more qualified applicants, and once they are accepted to a school, they realize success is up to them and their efforts. Students go to school to learn and succeed, not because they want to fit someone's idea of a diverse society.

These three letters reflect well the considerable debate over affirmative action, and they also reflect the fact that no one's mind will be easily changed about the issue.

December 27, 2004— The Met School, an unusual public high school in Providence, Rhode Island, was the subject of an article in the *Los Angeles Times*. The Met School serves 580 mostly poor and minority students. The school has no conventional required courses, no letter grades, and no tests. The students are led by "advisors" who stay with a group of students all four years, and the students offer "exhibitions" of their work in place of taking tests.

In spite of their poor and minority backgrounds, 100 percent of the senior graduates go on to some form of college. The success of the Met's "one student at a time" approach has caught the attention of other educators, and the Bill and Melinda Gates Foundation has decided to fund a nationwide network of similar schools known as the "Big Picture." There have been 18 Big Picture campuses established in the last two years.

The leaders of the Met School stress that it is not a panacea, but rather an alternative school for students who learn in a different way than in the normal high school environment. The Met School students spend time weekly in internships in local industry, and are in essence today's version of the "learn by doing" visions of the progressive schools of almost a century ago. Even though they have not gone through the normal testing routine of conventional schools, 75 percent of Met School graduates have some sort of college degree or certificate or are still in college. For these students, the Met School system worked. Of course, the necessary teachers to accomplish such results require special training.

January 2, 2005— Three articles in the *Los Angeles Times* published on this date addressed pressing educational issues. The first article bemoaned once more the poor results of American students in two international tests of mathematical competence released this month. When compared to other parts of the world, American students lagged well behind. The article pointed out in passing that it is not really fair to compare the average results from the huge school population of the United States, which features local control of schools and has extremely diverse school student bodies in both cultural and economical terms, with countries having relatively homogenous populations and tight central control of what is taught in schools. But the article urges, nevertheless, that the United States should do better.

However, many analysts continue to point out that putting access to schools ahead of the average academic performance of schools, which is essentially the practice in the United States, falls in the category of not being able to have your cake and eat it too. If public schools emphasize access to schools by everyone as a prime goal, it is basically a given that specific academic averages will fall below schools with more homogeneous populations and/or more restrictive educational access, especially if those schools teach subjects as directed by a central educational control. One must compare the basic goals of the schools in order to make an apples-to-apples comparison. Few, if any, countries match the diversity of the school population in the United States, while giving great leeway to local control of the schools.

January 2, 2005— The issue of local control of schools was addressed in one of three articles concerning education in the January 2, 2005, issue of the *Los Angeles Times* (one article is listed immediately above and another immediately below). The issue of local control makes it very difficult to measure achievement in connection with the No Child Left Behind (NCLB) Act. Specifically, the writer pointed out that children trained in California and Arizona would exhibit a great variation in degrees of math competence in the early grades if they moved from one state to the other. Other states would have similar problems. While NCLB stresses improvement over time, an influx of children from other states could temporarily distort results because different states have much different standards of what their younger students should learn and when they should learn it. This is another unplanned price that is paid to maintain local control of schools, and the writer feels it should be accounted for in some way when reviewing standard test results.

January 2, 2005— The third article in the January 2, 2005, issue of the *Los Angeles Times* concerning education (two other articles are listed immediately above) focused on the high failure rates in college of those high school graduates who do manage to make it to college. Over 60 percent of high school graduates go on to college, but 50 percent of these students fail to graduate from college with either an associate's (two-year) or a bachelor's (four-year) degree. The failure rate climbs to about 67 percent for blacks and Latinos.

According to the author of the article, Richard Lee Colvin, director of the Hechinger Institute on Education and the Media at Columbia University, these failure rates reflect the fact that today's high school graduates have the credentials, but not the skills, to succeed in college. In California, for example, the California State University system, the largest university system in the world (see entry for 1960), required 58 percent of its entering freshmen this year to take remedial courses in math or writing or both. Although these courses often fail to help laggards keep up in college (students taking one such course are twice as likely to drop out of school, while students taking two such courses rarely finish), students needing remedial work simply can't continue in college without it.

Colvin blames these results on poor preparation by high schools. Free and open to all, high schools turn out students who do not have the skills to compete in higher education, where costs and capacity essentially ration learning. But this is not a new problem. In spite of billions of dollars spent to open college doors for those who can't pay on their own, and in spite of efforts to beef up academic requirements in high schools, the percentage of college students who eventually earn degrees hasn't changed much since the 1970s.

At present, only two bachelor's degrees are produced for every 10 students who start out in high school in ninth grade. Less than 70 percent of ninth-graders actually graduate on time from high school, and with only slightly over 60 percent of these remaining seven high school graduates going on to college we are left with about four students starting out in college. Since only half of them graduate, we are then left with only two college graduates from the 10 that started high school in ninth grade.

Colvin advocates much closer ties between high schools and colleges. The Bill and Melinda Gates Foundation has joined other groups in funding Early College High School, a $120 million initiative to build small hybrid institutions affiliated with community colleges that after five years of schooling would issue both a high school diploma and a two-year associate degree, putting a four-year college degree in easy reach of students who have already been trained to do college-level work.

Another approach would have all high school students take the equivalent of a college-prep curriculum, and programs such as those that provide college scholarships to high school students taking harder courses, similar to those that already exist in Texas, Michigan, Georgia, and Indiana, would be expanded. The emphasis would be on providing courses in high school that truly prepare students for future college work.

January 3, 2005— The dean of the Boalt School of Law at the University of California at Berkeley wants to try to partly privatize the once-prestigious School of Law in order to make up for state cuts in funding. According to an article in the *Los Angeles Times*, Dean Christopher Edley, Jr., feels that the best way to return the school to its once proud position is to raise nearly $100 million now as part of a plan to eventually raise $300 million, a daunting task for a school whose last attempt at raising capital funds, in 1992, garnered only $14 million.

The bind Dean Edley finds himself in demonstrates how many colleges today, including very well-known ones, are struggling for funds. Edley feels that he cannot compete with colleges like Yale, Stanford, and New York University in terms of faculty salaries and still have enough for student financial aid. He wants Berkeley to have a big enough endowment fund to meet what he sees as necessary expenses without going hat-in-hand to higher-level administrators. The state funded 60 percent of the school's budget in 1994, but now it supplies only 30 percent. Edley, as many school administrators can tell him, faces an uphill battle to achieve his proposed changes and to raise substantial funds.

January 4, 2005— President Bush may have difficulty convincing Congress to expand his No Child Left Behind (NCLB) Act to the nation's high schools in spite of his recent reelection in November of 2004, according to an analysis published in the *Los Angeles Times*.

Presently, the NCLB Act covers testing of students in grades three through eight, and Bush has proposed adding testing in every year in grades nine through 11. Although many educators feel high school students need to be added to the act, the issue of underfunding of the present act raises questions about similar problems if the act is expanded. Bush's plan calls for $250 million to help pay for testing and $400 million for remedial reading and for programs to help identify students needing assistance at the beginning of high school.

Some conservatives feel the government is already going too far in "interfering" with the right of the states to conduct educational programs. Others on both sides of the issue feel the NCLB plan needs more flexibility. But with calls everywhere for improving the quality of the education students are presently receiving in high school, the NCLB Act is likely to expand.

January 12, 2005— Prompted by the need to do more testing under the requirements of the No Child Left Behind (NCLB) Act, some school districts in the Los Angeles area are now using numerical grades rather than the letter grades long in use, according to an article in the *Los Angeles Times*.

The numerical grades range from one to four, with four being the best. This system is replacing the old A through F system. The new system is tied to new state standards about what a student should learn at each grade level. The numerical grade more closely matches performance at the stated level. For example, a child reading well in class but reading at a third grade level in fifth grade will no longer get the B they once got. Their 1 through 4 grade will more closely match their performance against the standard rather than against a more subjective estimate of how "well" they are reading.

Similarly, such factors as attendance and classroom participation will no longer improve their overall grade, which will be based on their knowledge compared to state standards. It is hoped this approach will give a more accurate evaluation of what the student has actually learned, compared to the old letter grade system, which tends to be subjective.

January 12, 2005— President Bush made a speech in Falls Church, Virginia, about his plans to expand the No Child Left Behind (NCLB) Act to high schools, where testing would take place yearly in ninth, 10th, and 11th grades. At the same time, the President proposed $1.5 billion in federal aid to high schools.

The president noted that only two-thirds of ninth-graders finish high school within four years, and he complained that American 15-year-olds ranked 27th out of 39 nationalities in an international math exam. But some critics complained the current NCLB Act has been steadily underfunded by Congress, and if the act is not pursued effectively in the lower grades, additional efforts in high school will not help much.

January 16, 2005 — The *Los Angeles Times* carried an article describing how difficult it is to get into so-called "magnet schools," which offer greatly improved teaching and more resources than regular schools. The concept was created in 1977 as a way to achieve integration without resorting to forced busing. It was felt magnet schools would be so attractive that parents would be anxious to send their children there even if busing was required to reach the schools.

But restrictions on the racial mix at each school, and the limited number of schools available, have hampered the achievement of the goals of the initial program. The city has about 162 magnet schools serving about 53,500 students. But of the 66,000 applications in the past year, only about 16,000 new students were admitted. The worst — or most popular — case was the Performing Arts Magnet school, where only about 100 spots were available for the over 4,000 students who applied.

The magnet school program is hampered by the same type of problems that have affected many well-intentioned programs designed for public schools in large cities. It was originally designed to address a mainly black-white integration problem. However, three decades later, the Los Angeles School District is 73 percent Hispanic. Blacks account for only 12 percent; whites for 9 percent; Asians 4 percent; and Filipinos 2 percent. Ironically, the "minority" breakdown originally set to determine who gets into magnet schools often helps whites and Asians, who are more likely to go to college anyway, than it helps blacks and Latinos. Integration by computer, unless the database is constantly updated and the resulting criteria for decision-making are constantly changed, is very difficult to achieve, especially in large-city public schools.

January 20, 2005 — Lawrence H. Summers, president of Harvard University, apologized to a group of women professors for a remark he made the previous week that seemed to show that he believed there may be "innate differences" between male and female brains that prevent women from reaching senior academic positions in math, physics, engineering, and technology.

The fervor of the commentary over this politically incorrect remark brought to greater circulation a recent study at Virginia Tech on 224 girls and 284 boys ranging from two months to 16 years of age. Sophisticated electrophysiological brain imaging was used to show that the areas of the brain involved in language and fine motor skills (such as handwriting) mature about six years earlier in girls, while the areas involved in math and geometry mature about four years earlier in boys.

The result of this is that in coed schools, by age 12 girls think they're no good in math and never will be. Boys are "good" at math but poor at writing and literature. There is a great deal of overlap, of course, but girls generally lose interest in math and science just when they're about to become "good" at it. Some analysts say all-girl schools hold great promise for eliminating this problem. A study showed that 13 percent of the graduates of such high schools went on to major in hard sciences and math while only 2 percent of girls who attended coed high schools did so. Thus, a curriculum that matches the growth of certain brain areas would be much more beneficial to girls.

January 26, 2005— Ex-governor of California Jerry Brown, presently mayor of Oakland, California, gave a speech in Pasadena, California, to the California Charter Schools Association. He noted that the organization continues to grow (there were 512 charter schools in California at the time of his talk), and the concept still holds the greatest promise for the improvement of public schools in California in the future.

Charter schools are publicly funded, but are granted relief from certain state regulations in an attempt to improve student achievement through innovative programs and teachers. They are nonunion and thus are opposed by such organizations as the California Teachers' Association (CTA), a vociferous backer of unionism.

Brown actively backed and created two charter schools in Oakland: the Oakland Military Institute, opened in 2001, and the Oakland School for the Arts, opened in 2002. Both offer college-prep curricula and both outperform most schools run by the school district. Both of the Brown schools exceeded their growth targets on the state-mandated California Academic Performance Index last year, with the Military Institute scoring 628 and the Arts School scoring 753. The state's goal is 800, but most district-run high schools in Oakland average in the 400s or 500s.

Brown stressed that rules permitting charter schools to drop students not meeting their academic standards were necessary to make it possible for charter schools to meet their standards of performance. He pointed out that the No Child Left Behind (NCLB) Act imposes sanctions to keep schools accountable, and charter schools must keep their students accountable as well.

February 6, 2005 — An article in the *Los Angeles Times* pointed out that many parents of low-income minority children are trying to get into charter schools not only because of their potential to offer a better educational experience, but because they are perceived as being much safer than regular public schools in low-income minority areas.

There are only about 537 charter schools in the state's population of more than 9,000 public schools (with six million public school children), but nearly 60 percent of charter schools are located in the areas that serve predominately poor black and Hispanic students. Many of the parents of these children find regular public schools to be dangerous places filled with gang activity, and the charter schools stand out as beacons of relative safety while children are in school in such neighborhoods.

February 21, 2005 — *Time* magazine carried a feature article on problems teachers have with parents. Although many inner-city schoolteachers would welcome some sign of parental involvement with their generally low-income minority students, other teachers in other schools cite parents as their single biggest problem, far ahead of issues such as school funding or class size. Parent problems are given as a key reason 45 to 50 percent of new teachers leave the profession within five years.

The basic problem is often the concern of the parents with grades and test scores. Most parents can't — or don't want to — believe that their child is not especially gifted. The claim that a teacher gave their child a low mark, which is answered by the response that the student earned the low score, is guaranteed to touch off a conflict, especially among college-bound children, or among children already in college.

There is no easy solution to this problem. Parents who are involved objectively with their child's progress in school are a great help to their child and to the teachers involved with the child. But true objectivity is very rare. Parents typically want the best for their child whether the child deserves it or not, and the teacher is stuck in the middle of a no-win situation.

February 23, 2005 — A study from the Public Policy Institute of California showing the percentage of various young adult racial groups holding bachelor's degrees was released on this date. The purpose of the study was to show that young adults (age 25 to 29) born outside California earned bachelor's degrees at slightly higher rates than those born in California, but this effect was often overlooked because so many young adults move to California and thus the overall population in California had a relatively good percentage of people with college degrees. Actually, the differences were generally small for those born in or outside California, but the differences between racial groups were very large.

For example, 67 percent of Asians and 49 percent of Filipinos in the age 25–29 group had degrees, while 32 percent of whites did so. But only 15 percent of blacks and under 15 percent of Latinos had degrees. The percentage fell to just over 10 percent for Native Americans. Nationwide, the overall number of young adults with degrees ranged between 25 and 28 percent of the population. Many experts felt these differences were due to different attitudes toward education in the various groups that date all the way back to kindergarten or even before.

February 26, 2005— It was noted in an article in the *Los Angeles Times* that charter schools were getting a boost in expanding their facilities from a bond fund that was approved by California voters in the fall of 2004. Proposition 55 was a $12.3 billion state bond measure for California schools, but $277 million was specifically set aside for charter schools. There are long waiting lists for the popular schools, and the bond measure was aimed at helping the schools expand their facilities and build new campuses.

March 1, 2005— Bill Gates, chairman of the Microsoft Corporation and one of the richest men in the world, who co-founded with his wife Melinda the Bill & Melinda Gates Foundation, one of the world's biggest charitable foundations and one that gives large sums to education, wrote a special editorial in the *Los Angeles Times* giving his ideas on how American high schools can be improved.

Gates believes that our high schools are obsolete in the sense that only one-third of high school seniors graduate ready for "college, work, and citizenship." Gates feels that all students need to take college preparatory work in high school. They do not need to go to college per se, but if they do not take college preparatory work in high school, they will not be able to move into decent jobs in an economy that requires ever more ability by the members of the workforce. Those who claim that students who do not go on to college do not need a college preparatory curriculum, and, in fact, may be pushed to drop out by one, are wrong. Gates insists that all students need to be challenged more in high school because they are capable of better work, and if they do not get the proper training they will be at a major disadvantage when they try to enter the workforce.

Gates cites the Kansas City, Kansas, School District as an example. The district school population consists of 79 percent minorities with 74 percent living below the poverty line. The district had a high dropout rate and low test scores. In 1996, the district adopted a school reform model that, among other things, required all students to take college-prep courses. Since then, the graduation rate has climbed by 30 percentage points (other experts have noted that high dropout rates among minority groups is not necessarily because they cannot do the work but rather because they are incredibly bored in high school).

Many of the other recommendations from Gates are similar to those in the No Child Left Behind (NCLB) Act. He states we must constantly collect data about how students and schools are doing and intervene in schools that are failing. Otherwise, many children will never get a chance to fulfill their promise because of their "ZIP Code, their skin color, or their parents' income. That is offensive to our values."

March 7, 2005—*Time* magazine carried an article concerning the ongoing dispute about the reason for the lack of women in the higher levels of math and science careers in business and academia. There were many analyses of the difference in brain function between males and females, and many anecdotes about women whose careers were different than stereotypes would predict.

However, the prime conclusion appeared to be that most women followed career paths that have "traditionally" occupied women, but nearly any women who early on wanted to go into math and science careers did so successfully, with their major problem being both male and female naysayers telling them that what they were doing was not "women's work." With more women than men now making up the college population in the United States, it may simply be a matter of time and patience before women and men are represented in the appropriate percentages in all careers.

Some analysts point out that women have been permitted to enroll in many elite colleges (like the Ivy League) only since the 1970s and 1980s. Thus, drawing conclusions about the reasons for eventual career tracks for women is actually a bit premature.

March 9, 2005—PRIMEDIA (PRM), the leading targeted media company in the nation, announced that Judy Harris, most recently executive vice president of PBS businesses, would take over as president and chief executive officer of the controversial Channel One, the operation that reaches 8 million teenagers in more than 400,000 classrooms across the United States while providing news and currents events programming (and advertisements directed at teens — see entry for May 20, 1999).

The appointment was seen as a response to critics of Channel One who complain that it is purely a commercial enterprise with little educational background in its management. The announcement noted that the Public Broadcasting System (PBS) has excellent credentials in the area of education, and the experience that Harris brings to her new job at Channel One has been extensive in developing educational programming.

March 12, 2005 — On this date the "new" SAT was given for the first time (see entry for June 2002). The new SAT was intended to be much more of an achievement test on specific college-preparatory subjects than an "aptitude" test. In this way the test would be less subject to complaints that it was inherently biased against certain minorities, and it was felt the test would be a better predictor of how students would do in college. If the public schools through 12th grade attended by minorities did a poorer job of preparing them for college, the results would be clear in the tests, but that would not be a basic fault of the test itself. In theory, the No Child Left Behind (NCLB) Act would address the problem of bringing all public schools through 12th grade up to the minimum standards necessary for their graduates to go on to college.

March 23, 2005 — A Harvard University report issued on this date showed that the high school graduation rate from California schools in 2002 was much lower than previously claimed. In the state, on-time graduation rates were 71 percent overall, with 84 percent for Asians, 79 percent for whites, 60 percent for Latinos, and 57 percent for blacks (nationwide, the overall rate is 68 percent). In the huge Los Angeles School District, only 39 percent of Latinos and 47 percent of blacks graduated on time, compared with 67 percent of whites and 77 percent of Asians. The overall graduation rate is 45 percent.

The report added that California uses "misleading and inaccurate" methods to hide the poor graduation rates. For example, the state claimed an overall graduation rate of 87 percent, while the true number was 71 percent. The state countered that it is forced to use its methods by the federal government, and the methods rely too strongly on undependable data from individual schools (which receive funding based on how many students are claimed to be in attendance).

The gap in dropout rates between Asians and whites compared with Latinos and blacks follows trends that start early in elementary school. In Los Angeles, the majority of students who drop out do so between ninth and 10th grades. These students face a dismal economic future, and easily move into crime-related activities.

March 29, 2005 — The Supreme Court of the United States, in a 5–4 decision, strengthened enforcement of Title IX, the law that bars sex discrimination in schools and colleges, and that has become an especially controversial issue in sports. The Court ruled that individuals who speak out against such discrimination are protected from adverse effects of their complaints, even if they are not directly affected by the discrimination itself.

The case involved the coach of a girls' basketball team in high school who claimed he was fired in retaliation for his complaints that his team was forced to practice in facilities that were much poorer than those provided for boys. The ruling did not reinstate the coach but permitted him to go to court to try to prove he lost his job because of complaints of sex discrimination. Justice Sandra Day O'Connor said to rule otherwise would cause such complaints to fade away and not be brought forward.

April 4, 2005 — *Time* magazine carried an article on the honors program at Miami Dade College, one of nearly 400 community colleges (out of a total of nearly 1,200 community colleges in the nation) that offers an honors program permitting students a relatively low-cost way to get into the upper grades of an elite school like the Ivy League schools or Stanford after two years at the community college.

Minority students are especially attracted to these programs both because of their low costs and because of the fact that they can make the transfer to a more elite school without requiring some controversial affirmative-action-type help that might have been needed if they were an entering freshman. Higher-level schools seeking diverse student bodies also like this approach.

April 7, 2005 — Education Secretary Margaret Spellings announced changes in the No Child Left Behind (NCLB) Act that would give greater flexibility in the implementation of the act to states with strong accountability systems already in place, and which excel in the testing of disabled students. Spellings said that "it is results that truly matter, not the bureaucratic way you get there. That's just common sense, sometimes lost in the halls of government."

This statement was meant to answer the complaints of several states that federal standards have no flexibility for using state standards that achieve the same results and do not require replacing the state standards with federal standards. Spellings made her announcement at a meeting with state educational chiefs at Mount Vernon, George Washington's old estate just south of Washington, and it was generally very well received by those in attendance.

April 11, 2005 — Starting at 8 a.m. in the Eastern Time Zone, the results of the new SAT, taken on March 12, 2005, by 304,000 students, began to be posted on the Internet. The maximum score on the new SAT was 2,400, compared to 1,600 on the old SAT. The old SAT had two sections, verbal and math, on which a perfect score was 800 in each section. The new SAT had an additional written essay section on which a perfect score would be 800, thus giving the new total of 2,400 for perfection on the new SAT.

Of the 1.42 million students who took the old SAT in 2004, only 939, or about one student in 1,500, achieved a perfect score of 1,600. But for the new test, it will take a few rounds to establish what percentiles of students fell into what ranges of scores before each student will have a good estimate as to how he or she compares with other students on the SAT.

Colleges use other criteria than the SAT to determined who will be admitted to their schools, but there is no doubt that the SAT is one of the important grades in the consideration. In a world where last year there were 42,000 applications for the 4,300 spots available at UCLA in the West, and 17,000 applications for 1,300 spots at Columbia University in the East, every possible thing in the applicant's favor is crucial. Of course, if a student is applying at a school that is much further down the elite list than UCLA or Columbia, then the SAT score is much less crucial to the student's successful admission.

April 25, 2005 — As the scores on the new SAT taken March 12, 2005, were analyzed, it was found that 107 high school students, of the 300,400 who took the test, scored a perfect 2,400. This means about one student in 3,000 made a perfect score on the new SAT, compared to the ratio of about one student in 1,500 who made a perfect score on the old SAT (see entry for April 11, 2005).

It was expected that perfect scores on the new SAT would be less frequent than on the old SAT, if only because the new SAT is a longer test (a total of four hours) and contains more opportunities for that single mistake which would ruin a perfect score. Also, much depends on the particular version of the SAT an individual student encounters on the day he or she is tested. Still, administrators of the test were surprised that such a relatively high number of students, compared to the expectations of the administrators, got perfect scores the first time around. It will take a few years of testing to set reasonably firm expectations for future test takers.

April 26, 2005 — A proposal was introduced to the Board of Education of Los Angeles that the Los Angeles Unified School District (LAUSD) make it mandatory for all students to take a sequence of courses that would qualify them for admission to a four-year college in the state, whether or not the student intends to go to college. If the plan were adopted, LAUSD would join a growing trend in the United States to increase the rigor of the academic subjects students now take in high school. Proponents say the present job market requires such skills even if college is not in the student's plans. The states of Texas, Indiana, and Arkansas recently adopted public school requirements similar to those being proposed by the LAUSD.

Critics of the plan say more rigorous academic subjects will mean reduced exposure to classes such as music and art. In addition, they claim the already high dropout rate will increase. But the experience of school districts such as the one in San Jose, California, which introduced a similar plan five years ago, was that graduation rates actually increased by 10 percent. Students often drop out because they are bored in high school, and a more rigorous academic requirement helped alleviate that problem in San Jose.

The key point of the plan, say its proponents, is that too many students in LAUSD finally decide they want to go to college only to find they lack the minimal requirements. This new proposal would end that problem, assuming enough qualified teachers could be found to teach to the higher academic standards required.

April 27, 2005—An article in the *Los Angeles Times* highlighted a public school in one of the poorest sections of Los Angeles that, in the words of a UCLA admissions administrator, is a place "where you see all the things that people say you can't get done, getting done." The school is a magnet school (the King/Drew Medical Magnet High School) that requires all of its students to take "college track" academic subjects, and even though the majority of the students are poor blacks and Latinos, almost no one drops out. The graduates of King/Drew account for the most blacks accepted at UCLA, and the second most blacks and Latinos combined accepted at the University of California at Berkeley.

Having high academic expectations is a common theme at many successful inner-city schools across the nation, and the Los Angeles School District is now considering applying the requirement to all of its schools (see entry for April 26, 2005). Some high schools in Los Angeles routinely have less than one-third of their black students enrolled in college-track courses, and in the worst cases, the ratio dips below 10 percent. Even if the graduates of these schools wanted to ultimately go on to college, they would find they are not qualified academically to do so. This is one of the strongest arguments for requiring all students to take "college track" academics.

King/Drew also has other advantages. The school enrollment is just below 1,700 compared to 4,000 or 5,000 at many high schools. As a magnet school, the students select the school by their own choice (and that of their parents, leading to a school body with strong positive parental involvement). The key problem with many magnet schools is getting into popular schools in the first place. Further, there are twice as many girls as boys in the King/Drew school, a result administrators say is due to the fact that the school has no football program. This may be an additional message King/Drew offers for other schools looking to emulate its success.

At any rate, the graduates at King/Drew are in the enviable position of having representatives from the elite colleges they apply to, such as UCLA, come to the school and literally plead for those students they have accepted to their college to actually attend their college when they select which school in which they wish to finally enroll.

May 3, 2005 — It was announced on this date that psychologist Kenneth C. Clark, an important figure in the United States Supreme Court decision to end segregation in schools in 1954 (see entry for May 17, 1954), had died at the age of 90. The conclusions of Clark's controversial "doll test" (see entry for May 1951) were cited in the famous "Footnote 11" of the Supreme Court ruling that "separate but equal" was no longer viable as a concept in the United States because children separated from the mainstream by segregation suffered psychological damage that could never be undone. It was a great victory for Clark.

Ironically, by the time he died Clark felt his life "had been a series of glorious defeats." He was very disappointed at the long time it took for desegregation to take hold in the United States. His attempts as a consultant in the 1960s and 1970s to reorganize schools in Harlem in New York City (where he grew up) and in Washington, D.C., to be more favorable to integration were rebuffed. Perhaps the unkindest cut of all came in 1990 when he learned his old high school in Harlem had de facto segregation (all whites had moved away) and was rated as one of the worst schools in the state. He said then that maybe he really was "as naïve as some people said" he was. He was a hero to blacks in 1954, but he no longer felt heroic at the end of his life.

May 5, 2005 — Crossroads School, a prestigious private school in Santa Monica, California, joined a small but growing list of private schools that are replacing Advanced Placement (AP) courses with their own college-level classes, according to the *Los Angeles Times*. The courses are designed to help students get into the most selective colleges, and over 14,000 public high schools across the nation offer the courses. But many private schools feel the AP courses are aimed too directly at test taking, and do not help the students develop analytical thinking.

The effect of this decision will be small overall, because usually only private schools have the resources to develop such courses, and private schools represent only about 10 percent of the high school students in the country. But it is another example of how private school students usually have an advantage over public school students when it comes to being accepted at the most prestigious colleges.

May 17, 2005 — The Yale Child Study Center released a report that showed expulsions from preschool programs for behavioral problems were 3.5 times as high as those from elementary and secondary schools. Boys are expelled 4.5 times as often as girls, and blacks are twice as likely to be expelled as Latinos or whites and 5 times as likely as Asians.

The study was titled *Prekindergarteners Left Behind* and covered programs serving nearly 800,000 students in 40 states. Schools surveyed included public schools, Head Start, nonprofit and for-profit centers, and faith-based and other community programs.

Many not involved with classroom activities were surprised at the results, but the reactions of those so involved were mainly along the lines of interest that data had finally been collected to backup their experiences. The prime conclusion of most educators was that intervention and counseling must begin earlier than was previously thought to help children learn to succeed in school. The expulsion rate steadily increased with age, with 5- and 6-year-olds having an expulsion rate at least twice as high as earlier ages. Children in this age group are generally considered ready for kindergarten.

May 23, 2005 — In an article in the *Los Angeles Times* discussing "newcomer schools," it was noted that about 25 percent of the 6.3 million public school students in California are defined as having "limited English skills." Because the new No Child Left Behind (NCLB) Act emphasizes the use of English immersion programs in place of bilingual education, California has developed a number of newcomer schools to help implement the English immersion technique so that the students can be placed in the educational mainstream as soon as possible. These schools have been successful in easing the transition of these students to the English language, although some have been targeted to be shut down because they have not achieved their goals within the time frames permitted.

May 24, 2005 — The Los Angeles Board of Education on this date postponed a vote on deciding whether Los Angeles schools should all complete a set of rigorous college preparation courses, regardless of whether the students were planning to go to college. This is part of an ongoing battle across the nation to get more demanding academic subjects into the nation's high schools. (See entry for April 26, 2005.) One unique aspect of the vote was that a number of parents and children were demonstrating outside, clamoring for more college preparatory courses in the Los Angeles schools.

Proponents say that in other districts this approach has actually increased graduation rates because the students have claimed that one of their major reasons for dropping out of school was that they were bored. Opponents within the Los Angeles Board of Education say that half of the children in the school district already cannot meet less stringent requirements to graduate, and thus increasing academic requirements would cause more high school dropouts. Critics of this position, both in Los Angeles and across the nation, have pointed out that a reluctance to provide a higher degree of academic achievement in high schools because the students may not be able to pass the courses infers that granting diplomas to children who actually cannot meet minimum requirements raises the question of exactly what the diplomas are supposed to represent. These critics feel that a high school diploma should represent more than the fact that the child spent the proper number of years in school, often moving along only via "social promotion."

May 29, 2005 — In an article on the editorial page of the *Los Angeles Times*, Les Perelman, director of the undergraduate writing program at Massachusetts Institute of Technology (MIT), commented that the new SAT, which requires a 25-minute written essay portion, will not achieve the hoped-for results of getting new college students with better writing abilities, because of the way the SAT is being scored. Perelman feels that the grading instructions for the SAT pay too little attention to the content of the essay, and thus good scores are given to essays that really do not express either clear writing or accurate writing. Perelman believes that considering the fact that most good writing is rewritten rather than written, the emphasis of the SAT on five-paragraph essays written quickly to meet the time requirements do not accurately reveal the writing capability of the student, and giving the good grade simply for length is not justified.

Perelman recommends a number of changes, including the requirement of two substantial essays written over the course of a day. He also recommends having the tests graded on the Internet via a group of regional grading centers. But critics point out that the SAT is not designed to achieve a definitive conclusion as to whether the students can eventually write impressive pieces of prose. The SAT, after all, is simply an indicator of whether a student is more likely than others to succeed in school. Taking the test over the course of a day would be a logistical nightmare, and making the scoring process more complicated would make the whole process more complicated. The SAT, they claim, is not perfect, and can certainly be improved, but its use as an indicator of student talent must be recognized as being more important than stretching out and complicating the process in the hopes of making it an even more precise indicator.

May 29, 2005 — Teachers at Hollywood High School in California claimed that the pending decision as to whether to have every student in the Los Angeles School District take college preparatory subjects is not a feasible plan, because the quality of the students in the school system is much too low. The teachers pointed out that many students are the beneficiaries of "social promotion" and they quoted individual cases of students who had never in their high school experience passed a math test, but were moved along with the rest of the students, regardless of their academic performance. The claim of the teachers is that some percentage of the students are simply so poorly prepared that they could not possibly pass more rigorous academic tests.

It was noted that 85 percent of the graduates of Hollywood High School went on to college last year, although only half of that group went to a four-year university. The remainder applied to community colleges, where entrance requirements are minimal. Critics said the dichotomy of claiming that students are already doing so poorly that they cannot take more difficult courses, and yet pointing out that these students move on to higher classes and eventual graduation, once again raises the issue of what value a high school diploma actually has in such situations.

June 14, 2005— The Los Angeles Board of Education approved by a 6–1 vote a new academic plan to require all high school students to take a curriculum of college prep courses. The debate about whether to do so had been going on for months (see entry for May 24, 2005), and even though many teachers claimed students were unable to do higher-level work, a crowd of students and parents chanted slogans outside during the meeting supporting the plan, with some students shouting: "Give us life prep, not a life sentence." The president of the board, Jose Hulzar, said it was a grassroots movement of parents and students who felt they were being denied a chance to go to college that convinced him to originally make the proposal to the board.

The plan will take place in stages. It would begin with the class of 2008, with certain students, having parental approval, being given the chance to opt out. By 2012 all students will have to take the college prep courses with very limited exceptions. Los Angeles thus will join a growing nationwide trend to require higher academic achievement in high school and in turn permit more students to qualify to enter a four-year college.

July 14, 2005— Education officials in Washington, D.C., announced the results of the 2004 National Assessment of Educational Progress. The good news was that the nation's 9-year-olds posted their best scores in reading and math in more than three decades. In addition, the gaps between racial groups also narrowed.

Education Secretary Margaret Spellings credited these results to the implementation of the No Child Left Behind (NCLB) Act of January 2002. The Assessment tests were first given in reading in 1971 and in math in 1973. They have been given periodically ever since to 9-, 13-, and 17-year-olds. For the 9-year-olds in 2004 the reading scores were 219, compared to 212 in 1999, the last time the tests were given, and compared to 208 in 1971. The math scores were 241 in 2004, 232 in 1999, and 219 in 1973.

The results were mixed for 13-year-olds and 17-year-olds. For 13-year-olds, math scores were at their highest ever in 2004, a score of 281 compared to 276 in 1999 and 255 in 1973. But reading scores were 259 in both 2004 and 1999, compared to 255 in 1971, almost as good a showing as for the 9-year-olds. For 17-year-olds, reading scores were 285 in both 2004 and 1971, after a dip to 282 in 1999. Math scores were 307 in 2004, falling slightly from 308 in 1999 after being at 304 in 1973. The overall results for all ages were considered very encouraging by a number of officials.

The message is "that persistence pays off," said Francis Alexander, a member of the National Assessment Governing Board, which oversees the tests. Secretary Spellings said, "we've turned the Queen Mary" in reference to finally getting most scores to improve, but she added that "we have flat scores for 30 years for 17-year-olds. Flat is not good enough." Officials said that more attention must be paid to students in secondary schools in the years ahead. But the present results show that the NCLB Act is having a positive effect so far.

July 29, 2005— This Friday marked the end of a special four-week summer class (that was free to the participants) at the University of Southern California (USC) designed to help minority students, mainly Latinos and blacks, who have received scholarships to elite four-year colleges to succeed at those colleges when they enroll in the fall.

William G. Tierney, director of USC's Center for Higher Education Policy Analysis, organized the course to combat the problem that Latinos and blacks generally lag behind their classmates at such colleges and tend to drop out at higher rates. Even the students in the special class realized that although they were among the top academic students at their high schools, and had been recruited as minority applicants by colleges including Harvard, Dartmouth, and Stanford, they were not sure they were prepared to compete in such colleges given the questionable quality of their low-income minority area high schools. Some of the male students had been ridiculed and harassed for trying to get good grades in high school in such areas.

Similar courses have sprung up since the late 1960s, but USC is unique in that it plans to track the performance of its 25 students in their freshman year (when many minority students drop out) compared to the performance of students who did not take such a course in order to obtain statistical data on the value of these preparatory (not remedial) courses. USC places great emphasis on the ability to write at a college level because most of the minority students have their greatest lack in this area, and the course focused almost entirely on developing writing skills, including the vocabulary needed to effectively access the Internet.

August 4, 2005 — It was announced by the Educational Testing Service (ETS) that it was working with a group of colleges to develop a test to determine the "Internet IQ" of college students. A preliminary version of the test called the Information and Communication Technology Literacy Assessment was given to 3,300 students in the California State University system this spring to essentially test the test. Other schools involved in the testing are UCLA, the University of Louisville, the California Community College system, the University of North Alabama, the University of Texas system, and the University of Washington.

In the future, the test is expected to be available to take on a voluntary basis, and some colleges are considering using the test on incoming students to determine if they need remedial help. The project manager, Teresa Egan of ETS, said it is important for students to learn to use "technology in ways that require real critical thinking." Lorie Roth, assistant vice chancellor of academic programs at Cal State University, said that students have to learn to do much more than to "go to Google and get some hits." Roth added that knowing how to use the Internet is a skill "as important as having mathematical and English skills."

Fall 2005 — The report of the University system of California showed that every University of California school (as opposed to a California State University school) received more applications than the number of students they could accept. The University of California at Los Angeles (UCLA) received 42,103 applications, the most in the system, and accepted only 10,209 students.

APPENDIX 1.
BACHELOR DEGREES AWARDED
BY GENDER

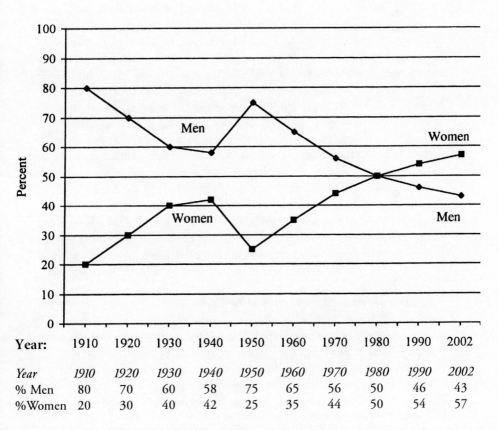

Year	1910	1920	1930	1940	1950	1960	1970	1980	1990	2002
% Men	80	70	60	58	75	65	56	50	46	43
%Women	20	30	40	42	25	35	44	50	54	57

The preceding graph shows the number of bachelor's degrees awarded in the United States by gender from 1910 to 2002. The graph shows that women only earned 20 percent of bachelor's degrees in 1910, but by 2002, they had overtaken men in the awarding of such degrees, and earned 57 percent of all bachelor's degrees awarded in 2002.

The percentage of women earning bachelor's degrees has been growing from zero percent around the middle of the 1800s, because women were not even permitted to be undergraduates in college until Oberlin College started the practice in 1837. Oberlin was founded in 1833 with the intention of enrolling women on an equal basis with men, but this did not take place until 1837. Also in 1837, Mount Holyoke Seminary opened as the first place of higher education for women only. Mount Holyoke then grew into Mount Holyoke College about 50 years later, but its founding date of 1837 made it the first of the "Seven Sisters." The Seven Sisters were colleges built for women only in the second part of the nineteenth century.

The Morrill Land-Grant College Act of 1862 produced a building boom in colleges of all types, and the newly freed slaves at the end of the Civil War created a need for teachers, as did the waves of immigrants that began to arrive in the United States on into the 1900s. It was generally agreed that women were best suited for the profession of teaching, and so their presence in colleges grew rapidly at the end of the 1800s. Thus by 1910, when the graph begins, women represented 20 percent of all college graduates. Women won the right to vote by the 1920 election, and from that date onward they started full participation in all realms of life in the United States. Accordingly they began to dominate the field of education as both teachers and students.

There were 50,000 degrees awarded in total in 1910. By 2002, the number was up to 1.3 million. The population of the United States was 92 million in 1910, and was about 293 million in 2002. This means that the number of degrees awarded in total increased by a factor of almost 26, while the population increased by a factor of just over three. This is a good indication of how both men and women greatly increased their enrollment in college during the 1900s.

The only time the total number of degrees declined in any decade was between 1950 and 1960, when the huge surge in degrees awarded in 1950 prompted by the creation of the G.I. Bill (signed in 1944) declined to a more "normal" level in 1960. But the number of degrees awarded in 1960 was still twice the number awarded in 1940.

The percentage of degrees awarded to women declined only between 1940 and 1950, due to the same surge in degrees awarded to men that greatly increased the percentage awarded to men in 1950 due to the G.I. Bill. From 1950 onward the percentage of degrees awarded to women climbed in every decade as the percentage awarded to men declined accordingly. As noted above, the total number of degrees awarded to both men and women was steadily increasing from 1960 onward. But women began to outnumber men in all phases of the educational scene, and the percentage of men receiving bachelor's degrees declined steadily after 1950. The percentage of men receiving degrees was just marginally ahead of women in 1980, and women took the lead during the 1980s. They have increased their lead in every year since.

As is detailed in the chronology, more women than men now graduate from high school, more women than men go on to college, and more women than men graduate from college. This trend seems likely to increase because Latino and black minorities combined make up an ever-larger part of the general population, and in these groups women far surpass men in seeking higher educational opportunities. It's a trend that starts early in the educational process.

The graph on page 151 shows clearly that one major feature of education in the nineteenth century, gender bias, was eliminated in all phases of education.

Appendix 2.
Students per Computer in
United States Public Schools

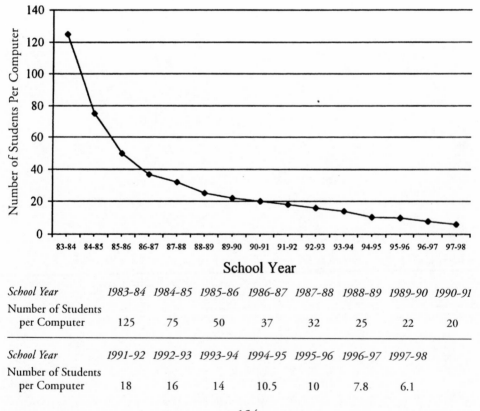

School Year	1983-84	1984-85	1985-86	1986-87	1987-88	1988-89	1989-90	1990-91
Number of Students per Computer	125	75	50	37	32	25	22	20

School Year	1991-92	1992-93	1993-94	1994-95	1995-96	1996-97	1997-98
Number of Students per Computer	18	16	14	10.5	10	7.8	6.1

The preceding graph shows the emergence of the use of technology in education by measuring the number of computers per student in the public schools in the United States. It also shows the recognition by school administrators of the fact that students in all schools must have familiarity with computers in order to hold decent jobs in the globalized economy of today.

The graph is one of those where a constant "decline" is very desirable. The personal computer was basically invented in the mid-1970s, and began to find its way into the educational process by the 1980s. A total of 125 students per computer, where the graph begins, essentially means that only one classroom in six had a computer. Today, one *student* in six has access to a personal computer, and this ratio continues to decline favorably.

In previous decades the use of technology in the public schools could be measured by the number of film projectors, then by the number of televisions and videocassette recorders (VCRs) and such items. Today, we use the number of computers and increasingly the number of schools "wired" for the Internet. Soon, the number of cell phones per student could be an indicator of the degree to which technology is being used to help students learn at all levels of the educational process.

A key trend is the fact that the students are learning to use the new elements of technology, as well as deriving information from them. When film projectors were introduced into schools their purpose was to provide information to the students in a new way, not to teach students to use film projectors. But with computers and the Internet, the purpose of their use is as much or more to teach the students how to use the items themselves as to provide a new way of presenting information. In the same way that students once learned how to use the library, they now need to learn how to use a personal computer and the Internet to find information and to communicate.

Some critics have complained that the use of computers in learning is too passive and students would learn more from field trips and such. But others point out that this complaint misses the point. The present need is for students to become familiar with the operation of a computer and the Internet, and the manner in which they can be used to find and present data and specific information. Even if some students never personally use a computer in their future work life, they need to know how it can be used for support in their profession or industry. Many will also use a computer in their future personal life to send and receive e-mail, to manage their personal finances, and in similar uses.

APPENDIX 3.
SCHOOL STAFF PER 1,000 STUDENTS IN CALIFORNIA AND UNITED STATES PUBLIC SCHOOLS

	Number		Percent	
	California	U.S. Average	California	U.S. Average
School District Staff	5.3	6.0	6%	5%
Teachers	49.3	63.3	53%	51%
Other School Staff*	20.9	26.3	22%	21%
Noninstructional Staff†	17.7	28.6	19%	23%
Total	93.2	124.2	100%	100%

*Other School Staff includes principals, guidance counselors, librarians, instructional aides, and administrative support staff.
†Noninstructional Staff includes attendance officers; health, psychology, transportation, social services, data processing, building maintenance, and security staff; and cafeteria workers.

The preceding graph compares the distribution of school staff in public schools in California, the nation's most populous state (having the most students) compared to the overall average in the United States. California has a public school enrollment of 6.4 million. Texas is next at 4.3 million, and only three other states exceed two million. The average for the rest of the states other than these five is about 0.65 million, roughly one-tenth of the school population in California.

Comparisons on a per student basis often seem unfavorable to large schools when compared to smaller schools, because smaller schools often need at least one person in a given category, while bigger schools can take advantage of economies of scale and have several persons in a given category service a large number of students. The same effect takes place in a post office, for example. A post office in a small town usually has more workers per resident than does a much larger town because the irreducible number of persons in a given category is always one. But such comparisons tell an analyst almost nothing about the quality of service.

The graph shows that California has about 25 percent fewer people per student on an overall basis. The difference ranging from 38 percent fewer in noninstructional staff; 22 percent fewer in teachers; 21 percent fewer in other school staff; and 12 percent fewer in school district staff (where the much smaller numbers of personnel mean people in each category tend to approach the irreducible minimum of one in many areas).

Teachers (with certificates) are the only nearly self-explanatory category. "Other school staff" includes principals, guidance counselors, librarians, instruction aides, and administrative support staff. Noninstructional staff includes attendance officers; health, psychology, transportation, social services, data processing, building and maintenance, and security staff; and cafeteria workers.

The comparison by percentage is perhaps more revealing. California and the United States average are the same within two percentage points or less except in the noninstructional staff category, where California runs four percentage points lower. This is an area where economies of scale would be expected to be greater in large facilities, and thus California would be expected to need fewer personnel. A lower number here would probably indicate greater efficiencies rather than any basic defect.

The most compelling number on either table is that teachers are just above 50 percent of the total "school staff." The U.S. average is 51 percent, while in California it is 53 percent. This means that the most crucial part of the education process, the interface between students and teachers in the classroom, consumes just over half of the dollars spent on personnel in the typical school system. Perhaps a good place to look for more money to spend on teachers, as is often proposed, is at the huge supporting staff that exists in our high schools (or at the regulations that require them).

California averages 20.7 pupils per teacher, while the overall national average is 15.9. This is a figure that can vary substantially within a state, with inner-city schools typically averaging higher and suburban schools averaging lower. California also pays the highest average salary for teachers, posting an average of $56,283 versus a national average of $45,822.

APPENDIX 4.
EFFECT OF TITLE IX

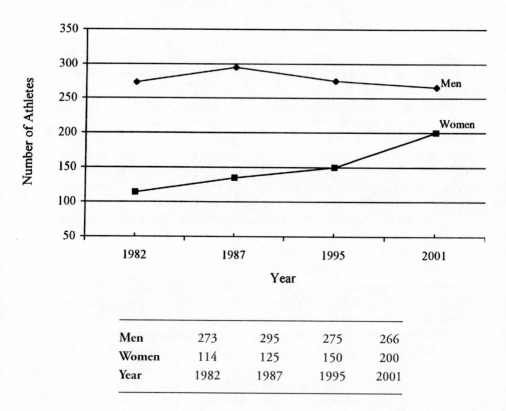

Average Number of Athletes per Institution

Men	273	295	275	266
Women	114	125	150	200
Year	1982	1987	1995	2001

Average Number of Sports Teams per Institution

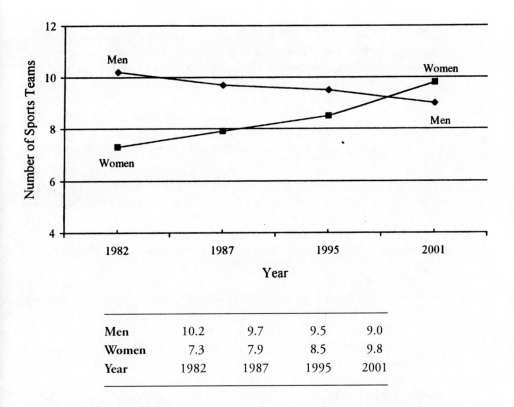

Men	10.2	9.7	9.5	9.0
Women	7.3	7.9	8.5	9.8
Year	1982	1987	1995	2001

The two preceding graphs show the effect of Title IX, the law that bars gender discrimination, on participation in college sports. Sports is the area that has generated the most debate over Title IX. This is because the argument that women's groups maintain is that if participation in sports is deemed to be a basic benefit of education, it must be offered even-handedly to males and females. This is an argument that is hard to refute at any level.

The basic sticking point is that sports teams, most notably in football and basketball, have become a source of revenue, especially at the college level. So-called student athletes in these sports at many schools are only "hired guns" to generate revenue for the school. Thus athletic directors (and often even school presidents) are loath to make sports budgets that divide expenditures equitably between men and women. The problem basically disappears at educational institutions that have not become dependent on sports as a key source of revenue. In many cases, though, athletics is a key consideration in revenue from alumni gifts because alumni have been shown to contribute more when their school is nationally ranked in some sport.

The first graph shows that women athletes per institution have nearly doubled between 1982 and 2001. For men, the number has decreased by a little under 3 percent for the same time period. This is not just because more women have been encouraged to participate in sports, but because many schools have cut the number of sports teams made available to men in order to achieve a rough equity between men and women. Understandably, men are not in favor of this approach. But women, who had hoped for more spending in women's sports, are not in favor of this approach either.

The second graph shows this effect more clearly. Between 1982 and 2001, the average number of sports teams per institution for men fell by almost 12 percent. For women, the average number of teams increased by almost 25 percent. The result is that women's sports teams per institution now outnumber those for men by almost 10 percent.

The United States Education Department uses the criteria that if the proportion of athletes who are female matches the number of undergraduates who are female, the educational institute is in a "safe harbor" in terms of withstanding lawsuits. Some proponents for men have argued that the number of athletes who are female should match the number of female undergraduates who express a desire to participate in sports, contending that fewer women than men wish to participate in sports.

This battle will likely continue for some time to come, or at least as long as some men's sports are seen primarily as a source of revenue rather than as an opportunity for male undergraduates to take part in team sports. Very few "typical" male undergraduates could be accepted as players on big-time football or basketball programs. The same is true for undergraduate females in institutions that play big-time women's basketball.

Some critics state that the issue will continue to be contentious until some clearer definition of sports as part of an education is made. If big-time sports is more like a business, with players "hired" to produce revenue for schools (which is presently the case in many schools), then perhaps it should be regulated (and taxed) like a business and set apart from the educational process regulated by Title IX.

APPENDIX 5.
STUDENTS ENROLLED IN
HIGH SCHOOL GRADES 9–12

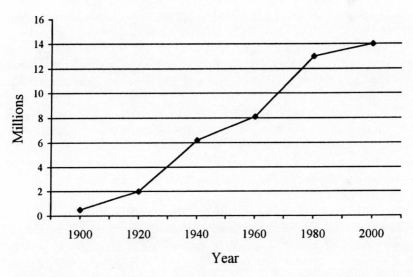

U.S. Population (millions)	Year	Students Enrolled (millions)
76	1900	0.5
106	1920	2.0
132	1940	6.2
179	1960	8.1
227	1980	13.0
286	2000	14.0

The preceding graph shows the number of students enrolled nation-wide in high school (grades nine through 12) since 1900. High schools did not become a standard part of the educational process until the end of the nineteenth century, but the number of high school students increased dramatically in the early part of the twentieth century. This was due to a combination of the pressures of educating the waves of immigrants arriving in the United States, and the fact that a high school education was becoming more and more common in the United States. In 1900 there were about half a million high school students, a number that grew about twelvefold by 1940. It more than doubled again by 1980, and stood at 14 million in the year 2000.

Comparing the growth of the number of high school students to the growth of the overall population of the United States shows that the rate of growth of high school students was about eight times as high as the rate of growth of the population between 1900 and 2000. But, as noted above, the sharpest increase was in the early part of the twentieth century.

In the 20 years between 1900 and 1920, the number of high school students grew by a factor of 4, while the population grew by a factor of only 1.4. In the 40 years between 1920 and 1960, the number of high school students grew by a factor of 4 again, while the population grew by a factor of 1.7. In the 40 years from 1960 to 2000, the number of high school students increased by a factor of 1.7, not much different than the 1.6 increase in the population.

As the number of high students increased in the United States, the issue of what curriculum was appropriate for them to learn also increased in intensity. In 1892, the "Committee of Ten" outlined an academic sequence of courses that ordered no difference between those planning to go to college (less than one-tenth of students did then) and those "preparing for life." All high school students were to take an equally high level of academics.

That approach was reversed in 1918 when the "Cardinal Principles" of education were released. They stressed that education should emphasize social integration and the building of values. This approach lasted into the 1940s, when it was reinforced by the "Redbook" report from Harvard, even though about 25 percent of high school graduates were then going on to college.

But the shocks of *Sputnik* in 1957, and the publication of the report *A Nation at Risk* by the Department of Education in 1983, brought demands for a much more rigorous academic curriculum in the nation's high schools, especially in the areas of math and science. Today the battle continues, with most high schools (and states) leaning toward a more rigorous academic curriculum in high school, including a requirement that all students take college preparatory courses regardless of their intent of going on to college (which nearly two-thirds of students now do), and a requirement for passing a graduation examination regardless of the grades the students were awarded in high school (where much "social promotion" exist).

The battle is especially strong in California, which has the highest public school enrollment in the nation. The No Child Left Behind (NCLB) Act, which requires more rigorous testing of children in grades three through eight, is at the center of this battle. A proposal is being made to extend such testing into high school through grade 11. The issue of the proper curricula for high school, which has been going on for over a century, seems sure to continue.

APPENDIX 6.
PERCENTAGE OF STUDENTS AGE 25 AND OLDER WHO COMPLETED HIGH SCHOOL THROUGH GRADE 12 OR GED

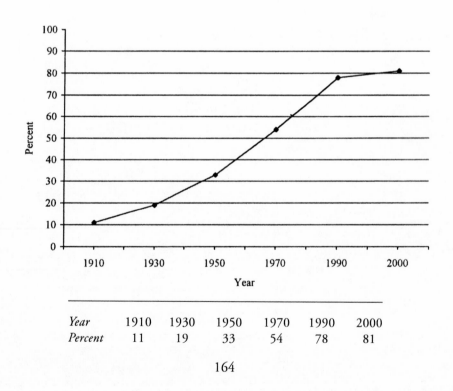

Year	1910	1930	1950	1970	1990	2000
Percent	11	19	33	54	78	81

The preceding graph shows the percentage of the population age 25 and over that has completed high school through grade 12 or has passed a GED examination. The GED (Graduation Equivalency Diploma) is legally considered the same as a high school diploma issued after completing grade 12 of high school. The graph shows both the persistence of some groups of the population in earning a high school "degree," and the care that must be taken in reviewing certain statistics related to education.

The "official" high school graduation rate nationwide for the school year 2001–02 was 68.5 percent, ranging from a high of 89.8 percent in New Jersey to a low of 49.2 percent in South Carolina. But this is defined as the number of students who enrolled in ninth grade four years ahead of the year being measured compared to the number of students who actually graduated from high school four years later. It is the "on-time" graduation rate, and it makes no adjustment for interstate migration.

The No Child Left Behind (NCLB) Act, which requires schools to show progress from year to year, has uncovered many "inventive" ways of measuring various "graduation" rates within a school system. For example, a study led by Harvard University found that instead of a state-reported 87 percent overall graduation rate in 2002 in California, the actual graduation rate was 71 percent, with the rate falling to 60 percent for Latinos and 57 percent for blacks. In the huge Los Angeles district, only 45 percent of all students graduated on time, with Asians at 77 percent, whites at 67 percent, blacks at 47 percent, and Latinos, who make up the overwhelming majority of students, at a dismal 39 percent.

State officials blame the discrepancy on outmoded formulas they claim they are forced to use by the federal government that rely on undependable dropout data from schools. The schools receive revenue based on their reported attendance, and thus their data is understandably biased toward the high side in terms of students reported as still in school.

In another case, a state was found to be reporting graduation rates based on the number of students who enter 12th grade compared to the number that actually graduate in the following spring. Since most high school students who are going to drop out do so between ninth and tenth grades, measuring only 12th grade dropouts gives a pleasingly high "graduation rate."

Efforts are being made to standardize measurement techniques so that real progress (or the lack of it) can be accurately determined. The data shown in the graph is "brute force" data and thus is more reliable than much data in the education field. It simply measures how many persons in the specified age group (25 and over) possess a high school diploma or its GED equivalent. The result of 81 percent is a very positive number in many ways. It says that of the 31.5 percent of persons "lost" to the education process when considering the nationwide on-time graduation rate of 68.5 percent, almost 40 percent of that group find a way to eventually become high school "gradu-ates." Presumably most of those discover that decent employment is hard to find without at least a high school diploma. Their persistence in gaining that diploma up to seven years after their "class" has graduated is admirable.

Appendix 7.
Education
Statistical Abstract

1. Percentage of 5–17 Age Group Enrolled in School: 90%
2. Percentage of Ninth-Graders Who Graduate from High School
   on Time: 68%
3. Percentage of High School Graduates Who Enroll in College: 65%
4. Percentage of All College Enrollees Who Fail to Graduate: 50%
5. Percentage of Black and Latino College Enrollees Who Fail to
   Graduate: 67%
6. Percentage of California State University Enrollees Needing
   Remedial Work: 58%
   Note: Those needing one remedial class are twice as likely
   to eventually drop out. Those needing two remedial classes
   rarely finish college.
7. Percentage of Ninth-Graders Eventually Earning a Bachelor's
   Degree: 20%
8. Percentage of College Enrollees Who Are Female: 56%
9. Percentage of High School Students in Top 10 Percent of Class
   Who Are Female: 58%
10. Percentage of Bachelor's Degrees Awarded to Females: 57%

The preceding table is a form of statistical abstract of the education process in the United States, listing notable statistics for different steps in the process.

The first statistic emphasizes one prime aspect of education in the United States: free access to all regardless of race, color, ethnic origin, handicapped or not, legally resident or not, and speaking English or not. Ninety percent of all children in the 5–17 age group in the population are enrolled in school. This is another "brute force" statistic that confirms that not only **should** most children in this age group be in school, they **are**, in fact, in school.

Few nations have a population as diverse as that of the United States, and with no restrictions on access to the elementary/secondary school systems, the school population here is basically more diverse than in most nations. That is why comparisons of average academic performance between schools here and schools in other nations must be made with care.

The second statistic is the "on time" graduation rate of the nation's high schools, i.e., the number of students enrolled in ninth grade who graduate from 12th grade four years later. As shown in Appendix 6, the graduate rate increases to 81 percent if one measures the number of students who eventually receive a high school diploma or a GED equivalent by age 25. As also discussed in the text accompanying Appendix 6, "graduation rate" is one of the most abused educational statistics, with many schools adjusting the method used to calculate the percentage so as to appear to have a higher number.

Statistic three measures the percentage of graduating high school students who go on to college. The number varies slightly from year to year, but it has held above 60 percent since 1990. At an average value of about 65 percent for recent years, the rate is about 10 times as high as it was at the beginning of the twentieth century.

Statistic four is a sobering statistic showing that fully 50 percent of the students who do enroll in college fail to receive a degree. Many analysts say that poor preparation in high school is the major reason so many fail in college. With social promotion (moving students ahead in school regardless of their academic performance), and great reluctance in many schools to increase the academic rigor of their curriculum (because of a belief more students will drop out), high school students are simply not prepared for college. These critics add that concern for damaging the "self-esteem" of students by requiring higher performance from them may seem appropriate in high school, but the self-esteem of the students may receive an even bigger blow when they fail in college after believing they were properly prepared.

Statistic five is a parallel statistic to statistic four. Latinos and blacks fail to get a degree in even greater numbers than the overall failure rate of 50 percent noted in statistic four. Their failure rate of 67 percent means that only one Latino or black in three who enter college will eventually get a degree. Poor preparation in high school, as noted in statistic four, is felt to be the main cause.

Statistic six supports the conclusion that poor high school preparation produces the high failure rates noted in statistics four and five. Statistic six shows that 58 percent of all students (well over half) admitted to the California State University System, primarily based on their high school grades, need remedial work, mostly in math and English, to even be permitted to stay in college after admission.

However, the college system is considering ending the practice of offering remedial work because the practice doesn't seem to help those needing it to eventually graduate from college. As noted, students needing one remedial course are twice as likely to drop out as students not needing any remedial work (and even a "normal" student has a high failure rate), and students needing two remedial courses rarely finish college. In essence, the students who need remedial work are generally so poorly prepared that they never catch up to their peers. Investing resources to do remedial work in an attempt to fix the failures of high school preparation is not feasible at the college level. Colleges have too many other problems that need attention if the college is to stay in business.

Statistic seven is essentially a result of combining the statistics listed in the items above. If we select 10 students in ninth grade, fewer than seven will graduate from high school. Of that number, only 65 percent or just above four will enroll in college. Of that number, fewer than half will earn a bachelor's degree (others will earn a two-year associate's degree), leaving only about two students with a bachelor's degree.

Statistic eight begins a group of three statistics that show the "feminization" of the education process. Forced to take second-place status behind males for nearly three centuries after the arrival of the founding immigrants in the early 1600s, women now dominate every aspect of the education process in the United States.

Statistic eight shows that 56 percent of present college enrollees are women. Statistic nine is part of why women now dominate college enrollees. Not only are more females than males graduating from high school, the females also are graduating with better grades. Thus, they are more likely to win college admission.

Finally, as shown in more detail in Appendix 1, 57 percent of all bachelor's degrees awarded today are awarded to women. Further, present trends infer that women will take even larger leads in all of these areas in the future.

BIBLIOGRAPHY

This bibliography lists the key books consulted in putting together this chronology. By far the most useful book and the one that addresses the subject of education most broadly is the *History of Education in America*, seventh edition. This book was written by John D. Pulliam and James J. Van Patten, and was published by Prentice-Hall in 1999. The book covers the history of education in America since colonial times. It provides much background and supporting material in addition to its coverage of the important facts and names involved in the history of education in this country.

Probably the best indication of the down-to-earth tone of what is essentially a serious textbook is the comment on page 188 by the authors that "one of the great tragedies of American education is that we keep inventing the wheel." The authors carefully discuss in detail the many times this phenomenon has taken place. They also correctly recognize how strongly various court rulings have shaped the form of education in this country, and they list the titles of many such court decisions. If the information contained in this book were carefully absorbed, a person would have a very good understanding of the history and evolution of education in the United States even if no other reference was consulted.

A good source of background material (and many period pictures) is *School: The Story of American Public Education*. This book, edited by Sarah Mondale and Sarah B. Paton and published by Beacon Press in 2001, essentially chronicles the television series of the same name earlier produced on the Public Broadcasting System. Many absorbing "human interest" stories are included in this book.

A careful analysis of the history of public education in the United States with a strong focus on the many "reforms" that have taken place in an effort to find the "ideal" system is *Tinkering Toward Utopia: A Century of Public School Reform*, by David Tyack and Larry Cuban. Both authors have written extensively on education, and the somewhat lighthearted title of their 1995 book sums up well their wry attitude toward the constant "reforms" urged by waves of "experts" to improve education during the past century. The attitude of the authors is similar to that of those who wrote the *History of Education in America* discussed above, in terms of how often "reformers" have attempted to reinvent the wheel. It is pointed out that only those "reforms" embraced by teachers as being actually helpful to their task ever become imbedded in the educational process.

An older book (published in 1983) that is still applicable today is *High Schools: A Report on Secondary Education in America*. This book was written by Ernest L. Boyer, who was a United States commissioner of education and later the president of the Carnegie Foundation for the Advancement of Teaching. His recommendations for the teaching of a more rigorous academic curriculum in high school would fit nicely into the debates today over what level of academics should be taught in high school. Boyer's advice is nicely buttressed by his comment on page 84 that "what is taught in school determines what is learned."

A very useful part of Boyer's book is an analysis showing that much care must be taken when comparing standard test results in schools in the United States to those of other countries. These countries may have a more selective process in determining who goes to high school compared to the free access for all system that applies in the United States. When only the "elite" scores are compared (those of the top 5 or 10 percent of the students tested), very little difference between countries is noticed. It's comparisons between the average scores of all students tested that show the United States lagging behind.

In addition to the books listed in this bibliography, great use was made of the Internet in developing reference material for this book. As the writing of this book took place mainly in the year 2005, it may be worthwhile to note that 2005 in many ways can be considered the 10th anniversary of the use of the Internet on a truly widespread basis. As noted by writer Andres Martinez, the "information superhighway" got under way in a significant way in 1995. In that year, Jeff Bezos began selling books online via what would grow into Amazon.com, the search engine Yahoo was incorporated, and eBay was launched. AOL (America Online) began signing up customers by the millions, but to some extent its future problems were foreshadowed by the first public offering of Netscape stock in August 1995.

All of this reminiscing simply supports the fact that the Internet in now truly a common reference source for a great number of people, including those who write books (and most who read them). The Internet is thus a recommended source of information in addition to the core list of books cited above. No attempt has been made to compile a list of specific Internet sources for this book because most references in the book based on the Internet are actually a combination of facts selected from several different Internet sources. Also, Internet information constantly changes as it is updated. Anyone interested in obtaining more information on a specific aspect of this book will be able to do so using the Internet.

Boyer, Ernest L. *High School: A Report on Secondary Education in America.* The Carnegie Foundation for the Advancement of Teaching. New York: Harper & Row, 1983.

Bridgewater, William, and Seymour Kurtz, eds. *The Columbia Encyclopedia.* 3rd ed. New York: Columbia University Press, 1963.

Butts, R. Freemand, and Lawrence A. Cremin. *A History of Education in American Culture.* New York: Henry Holt, 1953.

Hutson, Percival L. *The Guidance Function in Education.* New York: Appleton-Century-Crofts, 1958.

Knowles, Malcolm S. *A History of the Adult Education Movement in the United States.* Malabar, FL: Krieger, 1994.

Mayer, Martin. *The Schools.* New York: Anchor Books, 1963.

McGeveran, William A., Jr., editorial director. *The World Almanac and Book of Facts, 2005.* New York: World Almanac Books, 2005.

Mondale, Sarah, and Sarah B. Patton, eds. *School: The Story of American Public Education.* Boston: Beacon, 2001.

Nevins, Allan. *The State Universities and Democracy.* Urbana: University of Illinois Press, 1962.

Pulliam, John D., and James J. Van Patten. *History of Education in America.* 7th ed. Upper Saddle River, NJ: Prentice-Hall, 1999.

Tyack, David, and Larry Cuban. *Tinkering Toward Utopia: A Century of Public School Reform.* Cambridge, MA: Harvard University Press, 1995.

Tyack, David B. *The One Best System: A History of American Urban Education.* Cambridge, MA: Harvard University Press, 1974.

Welter, Rush. *Popular Education and Democratic Thought in America.* New York: Columbia University Press, 1962.

INDEX